LYNCHED
by Corporate America

LYNCHED
by Corporate America

The Gripping True Story
of How One African American
Survived Doing Business
with a Fortune 500 Giant

Herman Malone
and
Robert Schwab

HM-RS Publishing
DENVER, COLORADO

Although the author and publisher have made every effort to ensure the accuracy and completeness of information contained in this book, we assume no responsibility for errors, inaccuracies, omissions, or any inconsistency herein. Any slighting of people, places, or organizations is unintentional.

First printing 2007

Hardcover— ISBN-13: 978-0-9785094-3-9   ISBN-10: 0-9785094-3-9
Paperback— ISBN-13: 978-0-9785094-4-6   ISBN-10: 0-9785094-4-7
LCCN 2006925770

ATTENTION CORPORATIONS, UNIVERSITIES, COLLEGES, AND PROFESSIONAL ORGANIZATIONS: Quantity discounts are available on bulk purchases of this book for educational, gift purposes, or as premiums for increasing magazine subscriptions or renewals. Special books or book excerpts can also be created to fit specific needs. For information, please contact Herman Malone, HM-RS Publishing, 3840 York Street, Suite 200B, Denver, CO 80205, ph 303-308-3014.

www.LynchedbyCA.com

ACKNOWLEDGMENTS

I have to acknowledge the people without whose work, guidance, and advice this book would not have been produced: co-author Robert Schwab, of course; but also my ex-wife, Pauline, who lived through the turbulent and difficult days this book describes, along with my children, Leon, Miles, and Pamela, and stepdaughter Carie. I know I wasn't the most pleasant person to live with during this time.

Also the staff at my business, RMES Communications, who stuck by me even through the long writing of this book.

In addition, I need to acknowledge the patience and understanding of a dear friend, Donna Duplantier, who helped me through some very rough times described here; and I want to thank, too, the fellow plaintiffs in this case who stayed the course for as long as they could.

Finally, I want to acknowledge some people who have always been there for me: my loving sister Grace, my nephew Ronnie and his wife Judy, and some special people who will always be an inspiration to me, my grandchildren, Brandon, Jaclynn, Desmond, and Rudy. Lastly, but never forgotten, a very, very special acknowledgment goes to the loving memory of my grandfather, Bishop George W. Hunter; my beautiful mother, Emma; my Aunt Minerva and Uncle Dave; my late brothers, Lloyd and Thomas; and my late stepson, Rudy. They gave me the greatest gift they ever could, their love.

—Herman Malone

CONTENTS

FOREWORD

by Parren J. Mitchell

As a US congressman from Maryland, through the many years of my work developing an opportunity formula for minority businesses, there have been numerous occasions when it seemed almost hopeless to continue. But, nevertheless, we persevered to create a landscape where it became possible to address some of the economic inequities in the contracting marketplace. We refused to give up the fight for equality.

This book, *Lynched by Corporate America*, is a true story that epitomizes what occurs, all too often, in the courtrooms and boardrooms across America. Serving in the Congress during the Nixon, Johnson, and Bush administrations, we introduced historic legislation designed to eradicate such discriminatory policies and behavior, but as this book clearly illustrates, there is still much to be done.

The absolute courage it took to take on an international corporate giant cannot be ignored. This is a story, while regrettable, that must be told. If economic parity is ever going to be achieved in America, then racial discrimination must be confronted. Being informed and educated about what truly is happening is the only way justice will ever prevail. This book will certainly provide you with an unparalleled look into the accurate story of what unfolds in our court rooms—practically unnoticed.

It is only then that we offer up meaningful dialogue in addressing the racial barriers that persist today. There continue to be two classes of people in America. As the Rev. Dr. Martin Luther King, Jr. stated, "Injustice anywhere is a threat to justice everywhere."

The vital need to secure representation is essentially why I began the Minority Business Enterprise Legal Defense and Education Fund (MBELDEF). My organization, born more than three decades ago, was and continues to be necessary to assist in providing legal assistance and support to the many minority-owned businesses suffering the fate represented in this book.

This book is a must-read and should be a case study: 1) for students in colleges and universities across the country; 2) for businesses of all sizes; and 3) for people of all races. Its content should be eye-opening for our judicial system, one that professes to represent the fairness guaranteed under our Constitution, but which oftentimes remains blind to the reality of discrimination in the business world. *Lynched by Corporate America* will enlighten and educate readers of all ages.

PREFACE

by Herman Malone

My intention in writing this book has, from the outset, been to illustrate what happens in a courtroom when a powerful Fortune 500 company is determined to obtain the outcome it perceives as justice; what happens when one of the world's largest companies rules the courtroom with impunity while a judge in black robes sits on the bench giving his or her stamp of approval to what the justice system calls fair and equal treatment; and what happens when jurors who hear the cases are oftentimes oblivious to their own complicity in ensuring that Corporate America virtually always wins. At the turn of this twenty-first century, one company, Qwest Communications International Inc., formerly US West Communications Inc., was able to use its powerful influence to produce the results it desired from our nation's federal court system, all in the name of justice.

Never before in the history of the United States has there been a case heard like this in our federal courts: a business-to-business complaint of racial discrimination made against a megacorporation by a small business vendor to that company. This book is based primarily on the court documents that were generated from pursuing my case—specifically, a complaint that US West, which today is Qwest Communications, participated in a patterned conspiracy of discrimination against the few African-American business owners who contracted with the large company in the early 1990s. When a new chairman of US West essentially eliminated black contractors from the telephone company's supplier corps, several of those business owners approached me while I was serving as chairman of the National Black Chamber of

Commerce to complain of racial discrimination and disparate treatment, which even I had doubts about because I was making some pretty good money from US West at the time.

But my own company, as I learned, was definitely on US West's hit list. They simply had not gotten to me yet. This is the story of how they did.

Quite naturally, then, this book is somewhat autobiographical. It is based on my experience working with US West, the Mountain States' regional Bell Telephone Company, or RBOC, that was bought by Qwest in 2000, the year of the first trial of the lawsuit I pressed against the company despite cash settlements made with six of the original plaintiffs in the case. I was back in court in January of the next year, still pressing the racial-discrimination-in-contracting complaint. Much to the chagrin of Qwest, some extraordinary events allowed my story not to suffer the same fate as others. It was not filed away in boxes and stored in some lawyer's office or the warehouse of a losing small business. Instead, newspaper reporter and editor Robert Schwab joined me to work for five years to chronicle my journey through the courts, a tale that is guaranteed to capture your imagination.

This book has also been written on behalf of all those who have been frustrated by limited resources or legal technicalities that in effect restrain one thing our Constitution guarantees, the right of free speech. This book will illustrate how treatment of African Americans in the courts plays a pivotal role in denying a segment of our society equal economic status and helps perpetuate an abysmal inequality for blacks trying to do business with some large corporations around the country. My account also has been supplemented by interviews of a variety of principals in my story, from co-plaintiffs in the original lawsuit filed by the National Black Chamber of Commerce to jurors who heard the case in each of my trials.

INSPIRATION AND EDUCATION

My grandfather said when I was a little boy of nine, "Leave things better than how you found them." That thought has stayed with me throughout my adult life, and that's why I think this book is so important and necessary. If it helps in inspiring a teacher, a businessperson, a student, or anyone else to continue striving to make a difference in the world or to encourage perseverance, then I will have accomplished at least one of my objectives in writing it.

Growing up, I had some powerful influences in my life. My grandfather, mother, brothers, sisters, aunts, uncles—an entire community were always around to pick me up and send me on my way. Frankly, there were times when I wanted to throw in the towel and yield to adversity, but that would have been too easy. I always kept in mind how our ancestors never gave up when they faced even greater odds—and how often their very lives hung in the balance.

So giving up was never a real option for me. Regardless of how much pressure and doubt I faced, I relied on another of my grandfather's sayings: "Never, ever let them see you sweat."

Martin Luther King, Jr., another great influence in my life, once said, "If a man hasn't discovered something he will die for, then he hasn't got a reason to live." For God has a purpose for all of us, and I know I have been chosen for this purpose. My Lord and Savior has bestowed on me a wonderful blessing, and I am truly grateful. I bear witness that I am nobody without His strength. I am convinced that each of us has a mission, a role to play directed by the Almighty, and I'm not about to screw mine up.

TIME LINE

Fall 1969: Herman Malone is driven past a swamp near his hometown of Camden, Arkansas, and threatened by two white cops who say Malone might find himself floating dead in the swamp if he doesn't leave town immediately.

1984: US West is formed from three Bell Telephone operating companies to become one of seven regional Bell operating companies, or RBOCs. US West operated as a telephone company in fourteen states.

1989: Daddy Wags' Phoenix-based OJC Transfer and Delivery Service posts $405,000 in revenues.

1992: Dick McCormick becomes chairman of US West; African-American contractors for the company begin getting notices that they will no longer be doing business with US West. Malone receives notice that the company is planning to cancel his RMES Communications conduit contract with US West, two years into what Malone expected to be a five-year contract period.

1995: Research shows that US West, by this year, is spending just 0.33 percent of the four-billion-dollar total it was spending each year on outside contracts with black-owned businesses. US West argued that the 0.33 percent was actually 3 percent of $323 million the company had spent in total with women- and minority-owned firms that year. In September, 1-A Rob Moving, an African-American-owned business that had been working with US West from 1981 until 1992, shuts down.

June 6, 1996: The National Black Chamber of Commerce files a racial discrimination lawsuit against US West on behalf of four African-American business owners whose contracts with the telephone company had been eliminated.

November 1996: After civil rights leader Jesse Jackson involves himself in the case, Texaco, the large oil company, settles a racial discrimination lawsuit filed by its African-American employees.

August 1997: The National Black Chamber of Commerce holds its fifth annual convention in Denver. Herman Malone is chairman.

January 5, 1998: Herman Malone is deposed as a party to the racial discrimination lawsuit filed against US West.

February 1998: Ministers of the Greater Metropolitan Denver Ministerial Alliance announce their support for Malone and another Denver contractor seeking to join the racial discrimination lawsuit against US West.

March 13, 1998: US District Court Judge Wiley Daniel denies class-action status to the National Black Chamber's lawsuit; he removes the chamber as a plaintiff, but allows three new plaintiffs to join the suit. One is Herman Malone's RMES Communications Inc.

April 14, 1998: Herman Malone and his RMES Communications file for Chapter 11 bankruptcy protection.

April 30, 1998: Herman Malone is left out of private settlement conferences US West holds with six other plaintiffs.

July 8, 1998: Robert Knowling, chief operating executive of US West, who had argued to settle the lawsuit with the black contractors, abruptly leaves the company to join a West Coast technology firm.

August 1998: US West announces settlement agreements with six of the seven plaintiffs in the race-discrimination lawsuit filed against it by the National Black Chamber of Commerce in 1996. Herman Malone is the lone holdout.

January 1999: Federal bankruptcy court Judge Donald E. Cordova warns US West not to use the RMES Communications bankruptcy case to pressure Herman Malone into settling his discrimination case against the company.

March 1999: RMES Communications emerges from bankruptcy protection.

July 1999: Qwest Communications International Inc. wins a bidding war for a takeover of US West.

May 22, 2000: First trial of Herman Malone's race-discrimination-in-contracting lawsuit begins. It ends in a mistrial on the count of racial discrimination.

June 2000: RMES and Qwest, acting as a 50/50 joint venture, win the contract to operate public pay phones at Denver International Airport.

July 2000: Qwest closes on the merger with US West, which officially becomes Qwest across the telephone company's fourteen-state region.

January 2001: Herman Malone's second trial is held; Malone fails to prove his claim.

2004: Jim Robinson, owner of 1-A Rob Moving, an original plaintiff in the National Black Chamber lawsuit, and Robert D. Webster, one of the attorneys who represented the plaintiffs in the lawsuit, both die, before this book is completed.

May 24, 2005: RMES on its own wins a renewed pay phone and calling card contract in competition against Qwest/FSH and Verizon.

February 16, 2006: The thirtieth anniversary of the founding of RMES.

CHAPTER ONE

Media Day

Herman Malone was nervous. He was standing in a stone plaza in the sunshine—sweating on a cool day, he realized—at the entrance of the US West building in downtown Denver. His lawyer, Eric Vickers, an excitable man, stood beside him. Harry Alford, president of the National Black Chamber of Commerce, stood beside Vickers, and, together, the three men faced a huddle of reporters and a TV camera. An hour earlier, at the federal courthouse around the corner, they had filed a $150 million racial discrimination lawsuit against US West. It was the lunch hour. Workers were streaming from the granite skyscraper behind the three. Some workers glanced curiously at the group of black men and microphones and TV people. A few stopped to listen. Vickers opened the press conference by announcing that the lawsuit was filed as a class action, representing all African-American business owners who did business with US West. It accused the telephone company of discriminating against those black business owners, eliminating them from the company's lists of office supply vendors, construction contractors, and office movers who did work for the huge telephone company. Vickers said most of the black-owned businesses represented in the lawsuit had been loyal suppliers and contractors to US West for many years. He also said research showed that no other lawsuit quite like this one had ever been filed against a large US corporation. It was business-to-business, unlike most discrimination suits that charge an employer with discriminating against black employees.

But these black businessmen, Vickers said, owned small companies—businesses that hauled furniture and equipment from place to place in various US West cities; people who cleaned US West's office buildings; people who installed some telephone equipment, PBX systems, and switches, both for US West and other large RBOCs, the regional Bell Telephone operating companies that were spun off from AT&T when the federal courts split up the giant phone monopoly in 1984. US West was one of those spin-offs. It inherited from former Bell Telephone executives an already established tradition of promoting minority-owned businesses. That was one reason, Vickers said, the black business owners named in the lawsuit didn't really understand why US West was being so intractable with them, forcing them into federal court to redress their differences.

Jim Robinson, one of those plaintiffs and an owner of a Des Moines, Iowa, moving company, was there that day. "Herman had reason to be nervous," he said. "People in Denver knew who he was. If we were in Des Moines, Iowa, I would have been nervous, too."

Malone had other reasons to be nervous, yet he wasn't even conscious of some of them. He couldn't have foretold that day, for example, that because he was sweating there under the sun, he would suffer the breakup of his marriage, a bankruptcy that would nearly kill his company, and twice-told humiliation in court. His company, RMES Communications Inc., was the largest black-owned firm that did business with US West—ten million dollars in sales in one year. Malone, forty-nine at the time, had lived in Denver his whole adult life, having come from Arkansas after getting out of the Air Force at age twenty-one. He had built his business in Denver. He had even made headlines when he was unjustly accused in the press of fronting RMES for a white owner of the company. That accusation was nonsense, and state officials later cleared him of the charge, but Malone's reputation as a leader among blacks in business had been established by the ruckus and subsequent publicity. He was a founder of both the Colorado Black Chamber of Commerce and the National Black Chamber, and in 1995 he became chairman of the national group.

So standing up for black businesses and standing out in the black business community was nothing new for Malone. But standing up for blacks in a public square in front of the headquarters building of the very company that provided most of his business was another matter. He could lose money on this deal, he thought. Yet he didn't realize he would lose more than money. He didn't realize that his reputation as a businessman, as a black leader, and as a friend would all be questioned again as a result of that hour under the noonday sun. And it was not only his reputation as a friend to other blacks in the business community that would be challenged. His reputation as a stalwart proponent of all minority businesses would be questioned by other ethnic-minority business owners in Denver—Hispanic and Native American business owners who had, over the years, begun to work together with blacks to improve the business climate they all faced in Denver and throughout Colorado.

"I have not seen a company that is as mean-spirited and racist as US West," Harry Alford told the reporters. Alford was a big man, with big ideas for the National Black Chamber of Commerce—and for Harry Alford. Was he the black business version of Martin Luther King, Jr.? Harry thought he could be. He knew it took rhetoric—eloquent and colorful, but also tough and sometimes unrefined—to make the kind of national splash he hoped to make with the chamber. There could be big money in that. You don't have meetings with the chief executive officers of General Motors and Ford, American Family Insurance and Coca-Cola without having some impact on American business. And if you can get companies that size to contribute to your organization, you, as the director, can come away with some big money in salary and bonuses. He was called president of the chamber—that was his business title—but Alford thought of himself more as a CEO. He was certainly as much of a business leader in his own mind as were the people with whom he met to solicit funds for the chamber.

Vickers was another story. Alford and Malone knew Vickers, a St. Louis lawyer, from working with him in Washington, D.C., primarily with a group led by former Maryland congressman Paren Mitchell and the Minority Enterprise Legal Defense and Education Fund. Vickers had a flare for taking on powerful interests. He seemed to enjoy standing up to them. He had taken on the contractors' case with a fire in his belly. Now he told the Denver reporters that the National Black Chamber and two of the plaintiff companies—1-A Rob Moving Inc., Robinson's company in Des Moines, and OJC Transfer & Delivery Inc., owned by Jim Wagoner in Phoenix, Arizona—were taking on US West because all African-American businesses in the telephone company's fourteen-state service area had been plainly discriminated against.

For two years since 1994, Jim Robinson, the owner of 1-A Rob, and Jim Wagoner, who had started OJC Transfer after being encouraged by US West dispatchers, had been trying desperately to get back some of the business they had once performed for US West. Their companies were dying without it. But each man, Vickers said, had been denied an opportunity to return to work for US West—and the refusal of US West to work with them again was simply because they were black. "The denial of contracting opportunities to plaintiffs OJC and Rob Moving is part of a pattern and practice of US West to deny contracts to African-American businesses," Vickers read from the lawsuit. "Plaintiffs OJC and Rob Moving have been directly victimized by US West's trend of denying and decreasing contract opportunities for African-American businesses."

That exclusion, Vickers said, was intentional. US West employees and the people who ran its contracting subsidiary, US West Business Resources Inc., no longer wanted to have anything to do with black contractors. It was true, Vickers said, that the company's officers and managers were consolidating their entire supplier corps, company-wide. But there had been a change of leadership at US West in 1992, the year the blacks started losing their business, and now, what the new managers at US West were telling black businessmen was that blacks were no longer good enough to do business with it. No longer big enough; no longer efficient enough; no longer cheap enough. Blacks and other small suppliers were costing the telephone company a whole lot of money, and competition was rough in the telecommunications market. US West could no longer afford to do business with companies that couldn't offer them the lowest price or the best service; and so US West wasn't any longer going to do business with those companies. It was a coincidence, regretfully, that so many of those businesses were owned by blacks.

Alford stepped up to the microphone again. Black business owners and the black community, he said, suffered a trade imbalance with US West, and it was crippling black communities across the entire region. US West sold its telecommunications services to African-American consumers and business people from Arizona to North Dakota and from Seattle to Omaha, and those US West customers, black though they might be, paid their telephone bills just like white folks who were customers of the giant company. Those blacks represented millions of dollars that US West collected every month, year after year. So instead of kicking blacks off the roster of companies US West did business with, the company should be giving back to the black community like other Baby Bells in other parts of the country. In fact, US West should be spending at least a billion dollars a year—especially with black contractors like Jim Robinson and Jim Wagoner—to balance out the community equation. But instead, US West was spending just a pittance with black businesses—one-third of 1 percent of its business spending to be exact. One-third of 1 percent! Alford shouted. That's 0.33 percent of US West's four billion dollars in outside business-to-business contracting in 1995. That's an outrage, Alford said. A disgrace!

* * *

Although he was sweating, Herman thought things were going well. Jim Robinson and Jim Wagoner were sitting on the low wall that swept away from the doors of the US West building, almost invisible to the reporters and everyone else in the square. Invisible men, Herman thought with a chuckle, remembering Ralph Ellison. But as for himself, he added mentally—Herman Malone was anything but invisible. He was high profile; he was out there, as he always had been, over and over again in his career.

* * *

Malone, Robinson, and Wagoner had agreed that Vickers and Alford should do the talking at the press conference, but all of the men who organized the event wanted Herman out front during the session for a reason. Some of the Denver reporters might know him, they all argued; he was the chairman of the National Black Chamber, and, therefore, a symbol of black business leadership. But as he stood there, Malone could think of only one thing: here we go again; nothing has changed.

He remembered driving past the swamps outside his hometown of Camden, Arkansas, with two white cops who said he was going to be lucky that night because there were a lot of other niggers not so lucky who were still out in that swamp, niggers whose bodies were rotting under the surface of the watery graveyard. Niggers who hadn't been so lucky as he was, they said. They were going to let him go as long as he promised to leave town that night. They didn't want any troublemakers around Camden. When Herman had gotten up on the hood of a car outside a nightclub where the two cops were arresting two black men for a scuffle, they had come for Malone instead because they could always arrest the other two blacks later. Camden wouldn't put up with an agitator who could get other blacks all riled up. That was his mistake, one of the cops said. But he also said he knew Lloyd, Herman's older brother, and he liked Lloyd, so they were going to trust Herman to pack up quickly and get out of town.

That's how Herman had come to Denver. Just out of the Air Force, back from Germany—he hadn't even received his last military paycheck—and here he was being kicked out of his own hometown. He told his mother to send the check to his sister Grace. She was brokenhearted and dumbfounded over his leaving, but he didn't want to tell her why he had to leave so suddenly. He just had to hurry and get out of there. So send the check to Gracie's house in Lawton, Oklahoma, he told her. Then he did get out of town. And in short order, he was in Denver. He met a friend, someone from the service, who told Herman there was opportunity in Denver. He worked at Montgomery Ward for a while and then started his own electrical supply business. Now, he was standing here wondering how long it would take US West to make him just as broke as Wagoner and Robinson. How long would it take, he thought, to cancel all his business, too? He had already dropped from doing ten million dollars in annual sales with US West to one million dollars. They might as well lynch him, he thought, or drown him in a swamp. That would certainly have been faster, not like the slow business death they were putting him, RMES, and his family through now.

$$* \quad * \quad *$$

Eric Vickers was still talking. He claimed that each of the plaintiffs—in fact, every other black contractor who was a victim of US West's discrimination—deserved fifty million dollars in damages to compensate for their losses: ten million dollars in actual damages to redress the discrimination that was threatening the lives of each of their businesses and at least forty million dollars each in punitive damages, to send US West a clear message that black communities would not put up with the company's exclusionary policies.

$$* \quad * \quad *$$

"How did it come to this?" Herman wondered. It was unsettling, regrettable. Personally, he didn't like doing business like this, going to court and all. But he also knew from the sixties and seventies, from when he was in Camden, that black civil rights issues always landed in court. Harry Alford, Robinson, Wagoner, and Herman had all thought US West would negotiate with them, come to some kind of settlement, reach some agreement, and put the black businesses back to work. But that hadn't happened. They had written to Sol Trujillo, US West's president and the number-two executive in the company—someone Herman knew personally. They wrote him twice, but Sol didn't even answer the letters. So here they were, on US West's steps, after filing the lawsuit around the corner at the federal courthouse. "How else are we going to get their attention?" Herman thought.

* * *

Jeff Garrett, a man who identified himself as a US West representative, approached the speakers and the cameras. Robinson and Vickers remembered later that Garrett wore mirror sunglasses, the dark silvery shades like the ones you see in movies hiding the eyes of characters who play tough, bigoted state troopers.

Garrett was livid.

"Outrageous," he declared to the reporters.

The accusations made in the lawsuit were an insult to US West and every one of the company's fifty thousand employees, Garrett said—including the many blacks who worked for the company, some of whom were standing right there, listening. US West doesn't discriminate, he said. It doesn't discriminate against its own employees; it doesn't discriminate against black vendors; it doesn't discriminate against Hispanics or Native Americans or anybody. The company has a reputation for supporting ethnic communities. It supports its customers of color because that's just good business. US West's president was Sol Trujillo, a Hispanic. The Hispanic community looked up to Sol Trujillo, as did all of US West's suppliers. Sol was well known in Denver; he was well known in all of Colorado; he was well known in Omaha, Phoenix, and Seattle. He and the company were admired for US West's minority-enterprise programs, Garrett said. US West had been working with Colorado minority business owners and women business owners for years, and, in fact, had spent $323 million with women and minority firms during 1995 alone. He had the figures right there with him as he spoke. And more than 3 percent of the $323 million had been spent with black firms, African-American firms, he added.

* * *

Afterward, Robinson said Garrett had seemed to be making points with the reporters. They had begun to listen and to take everything he said down in their notebooks. Garrett turned to Vickers as he spoke, and Robinson said he seemed to be talking down to the lawyer, condescending. Robinson could tell Vickers was getting a little hot under the collar. Garrett was getting under his skin and stealing his show.

Garrett, Robinson said, acted like the contractors' claims were frivolous, as if they could have no gripes at all—like the whole scene was a scam—and the reporters would be foolish not to recognize that. Suddenly, Vickers rose to the bait.

"You could take those glasses off," Vickers said, "and look me in the eye and say that."

"I don't have to take my glasses off," Garrett told him.

"Then get out of my face," Vickers told the sunglasses.

"It was tense," Malone recalled. "It was emotional."

But the reporters were enjoying the show. It was a good story—one you don't get very often—with both sides arguing it out on the street before a building that houses a company being accused of serious charges. Garrett made his points, but the black men also made theirs, and the cameras rolled.

* * *

Yet Malone was still troubled. He was willing to stand up, to bring the national chamber into this issue, because it was an important one. But he couldn't understand why US West, the same company that had made him its largest outside African-American contractor, wouldn't agree to meet with him, Robinson, or Wagoner to work out their problems. The country was embroiled even then in a debate over the future of affirmative action. A white highway contractor from Colorado had actually filed a lawsuit that was making waves in the minds of government officials about whether it was proper for a large company or the state to concern itself with making sure that minority-owned companies got some of the business that they do with outsourced vendors. When

Robinson and Wagoner and other black contractors had approached Malone as new chair of the national chamber, Herman didn't believe them at first. He didn't believe that US West was systematically taking business away from them and handing it to other firms—not black firms, but other Hispanic- and white-women-owned firms, and even some white male firms. He didn't believe that US West was actually eliminating its black contractors from its vendor base. But then Malone realized it was happening to him, too.

It had started back in 1992, when US West signaled it was going to renege on Malone's ten-million-dollar conduit-supply contract. Malone had already spent many of those millions to buy a warehouse building in Denver and to set up equipment-management facilities in several states across the country. It was this contract that was the meat and potatoes of his company, providing 85 percent of his total business, and the pride of RMES. Yet standing there under the sun, out front as usual, he was now fighting desperately with US West for just a fraction of that business. His US West revenues had dropped to just one million dollars. The company had wrangled with him for the past three years trying to talk him into changing the focus of his work with them, trying to convince him instead to become a construction contractor for US West and dig ditches for it rather than being a distributor and parts supplier to the company, which was the industry that Malone knew. He could stand up, he thought, watching this show, listening to Vickers bicker with the US West man, Garrett, over Garrett's sunglasses, over discrimination, and over US West's commitment to the black community. However, what it all would come down to, he knew, was whether he had the money in his company to survive, whether he was making enough money in the company to provide for his family and leave something to his sons and daughter. He could imagine Garrett riding up the elevators in the skyscraper behind him with his report to US West's public relations department. Garrett could say their very own poster boy for minority enterprise was standing out there in front of their headquarters building haranguing the company's record with black customers and black suppliers. Malone wondered again how and why it had come this far. Not after the sixties and seventies. Not after building his business into a ten-million-dollar concern, he thought. But even after it all, when he looked back at why he was there, he thought once again, nothing had changed. He might as well have been standing in the dark at the edge of that swamp. Nothing had really changed. Nothing.

CHAPTER TWO

The Plaintiffs

In Denver he was called Daddy Wags. People knew him because he would call in to a radio show to talk Bronco football—an obsession for him. Listeners seemed to like what he had to say, and the talk-show hosts enjoyed his analysis. But Jim Wagoner was more than someone who just ragged on the radio. He held a master's degree in counseling, taught college psych for eleven years, and was a one-time administrator at a metro Denver community college. That's why many people who heard Daddy Wags on the radio really knew him as a teacher and counselor. Then he moved to California. He was actually following his wife's career then. She was a librarian, and as she moved to jobs in California and then Arizona, Wagoner started driving a delivery truck for a friend who did contract hauling for AT&T in Phoenix. After some people in the dispatch offices of US West there said they could use a good truck driver like him, he thought about going into business for himself. "We like your work," Wagoner said they told him. So he thought about becoming an entrepreneur. Then he started OJC Transfer and Delivery Service.

That was 1987, and OJC did pretty well. The US West people were right. They used OJC a lot. By 1989 the company posted annual revenues of more than $405,000. The next year was even better. OJC posted more than a half million in sales—$53,000 more than a half million. Daddy Wags was on a roll. But late that year, US West started using a new hauler, Express Courier, a company Wagoner learned was run by some friends of one of the US West transportation managers in Phoenix. At the same time, one of Wagoner's friends at the company, Art

Hidalgo, was promoted to a position in Denver. The next year, 1991, OJC saw its sales drop to $360,000, considerably less than half a million. So by August of that year, Wagoner wrote to Hidalgo in Denver that OJC was seeing less and less work since Phoenix had begun using Express Courier. He said he had asked the dispatcher "whether there was anything wrong with our service or our rates, or had there been any complaints about our employees." But "we were given assurances that none of these areas were problems and that our work was very good," he wrote. Dispatchers also told OJC that all US West vendors' work was being cut back.

In early 1992 Wagoner received a letter from US West announcing a new company policy. At first it didn't sound like good news. Across all of US West's fourteen states, the letter said, the company was reducing the number of its outside contractors and its vendor suppliers, by a whopping 85 percent. It was calling this its Interlog program. US West had to cut costs, and Interlog was a plan to consolidate all US West outside suppliers, reducing the number to a select few. But vendors who survived would become that much more important to the company. US West hoped it could get some price concessions from those contractors because of the increased volume the suppliers would handle, but that was another aspect of the cost-cutting program.

Now 85 percent is a pretty drastic number, and it would have caused most people who were doing business with US West to worry. OJC had done well since it started, but it had done well because of its business with US West. Those big numbers it posted in 1989 and 1990 were mostly US West business, and the company still accounted for 80 to 90 percent of OJC business even as those revenues fell in 1991. That's why Express Courier hurt Wagoner so much. It was winning more and more business from OJC's largest customer, taking it away from OJC.

But even as the Interlog letter arrived, Wagoner got a call from Phil Nearing, the US West manager who wrote it. Nearing said OJC was one of the few suppliers to survive the cut. "You are one of the percentage that is left to get business from US West," Nearing told him. "Those of us left would be getting more business," Wagoner said. But it never happened. Not for OJC. In 1992, revenues fell off precipitously, to just

$166,600. And it wasn't as if Wagoner didn't realize that was happening. By May of that year he wrote to Peggy Milford about it. She was the chief of US West's Business Resources unit, one of the big cheeses for whom Wagoner and all other minority suppliers of the company worked. "The demise of OJC continues as of April 27, 1992," Wagoner wrote. But the letter did no good. OJC still finished the year doing a little more than a quarter of the business it had done with US West in 1990. Daddy Wags wondered, "What's up with that?"

* * *

Jim Robinson was also a truck driver. He started his company, 1-A Rob Moving, in Des Moines and began hauling furniture and other equipment for US West in 1981. He was a burly, stocky, dark-skinned black man who liked to talk. He was emotional at times and perhaps not the best businessman—perhaps not the best businessman a lot of the time. He did business on a handshake; in depositions, he told US West attorneys he had always thought US West would treat him fairly and keep him working if he did good work for the company at a fair price. "As long as we served with dignity, respect, and price, and did a good job, we would always have our work," he said. "If we done a good job, we would be there."

Larry Theis, US West's outside counsel—B. Lawrence Theis of the Denver office of the law firm Perkins Coie—asked Robinson during a deposition, "Forever? You thought you would have the work forever?"

"If they needed us, yes," Robinson said.

"Even if someone came along with a better price?" Theis asked.

"No one had a better price," Robinson told him. "We made sure of that."

And that's who Jim Robinson was.

"An all-around good guy," Malone said later. "A solid person—he's the type of person you would get into a foxhole with. You can count on him." And US West had counted on Jim Robinson. He hauled furniture and moved office equipment from place to place across Des Moines. He backed up construction crews by restoring landscaping that was disturbed when workers installed telephone lines. 1-A Rob worked for US West for fifteen years, and for the first ten of them, Robinson thought US West was a great company. He was growing year to year and made as much as $108,000 with US West in 1991. He was building up his business with other companies, too, but US West managers in Des Moines made it clear they wanted 1-A Rob drivers to be available when something had to be done. So the phone company got Robinson's top priority. "You were our bread and butter," he said. "We were on call with US West. We made you our main concern. If somebody else was to call, I wouldn't take their work, so I could do your work."

Like Jim Wagoner, Robinson got Phil Nearing's letter in February of 1992. Robinson said he had had some earlier problems with US West when managers insisted that he procure some required licenses, and he had hired an attorney to help him work out those problems. But he said his real difficulty with US West began with the Nearing letter because it was then that his business with the telephone company began to drop off dramatically. And business fell, even though—just like with Wagoner—Nearing in Denver and other US West people in Des Moines assured him it would not.

During depositions, Theis, US West's lawyer, found that Robinson was a hard man to pin down. First, his memory wasn't so good. It ran events and dates together, and when Theis asked Robinson about 1995, Robinson responded about something that happened in 1992. Robinson also was antagonistic. He treated the corporate lawyer as if Theis really were some kind of shark, trolling Robinson's memory for anything that might betray Robinson's version of the way he felt US West had treated him. Robinson was convinced US West had treated him badly. "I believe that in 1992 when the changes were made at the top of the [US West executive] ladder, things changed for black minority contractors," he said. "Black contractors specifically."

"It had to come from the top," he told the lawyers. "Because too many of us suffered the same fate at the same time. And when we complained about it, it fell on deaf ears—with everybody we complained to."

During those depositions, as Theis continued to interrupt or contradict him, Jim Robinson finally began to snap. "Damn it," he said angrily. "Shut up! Damn it."

Robinson felt truly aggrieved. He had been working for US West for more than a decade when the Nearing letter told him the company was going to cut back the number of its suppliers through Interlog. But then Nearing told him he'd be okay. Another US West manager, Art Hidalgo, held a meeting in Des Moines where he discussed how Interlog was going to work. Robinson brought his drivers to the session and sat through the long explanation of how scanners were going to help drivers better track the materials they brought back and forth in their trucks. Then Hidalgo started to hand out the scanners to the various companies in attendance. When he got to Robinson and his drivers, however, he had none left.

"Now, this is work we had been doing all along," Robinson said. "We pioneered the routes in Iowa. We ran it for several years. We worked out the kinks in it…[but] all of a sudden other carriers were taking our routes…."

"Hidalgo passed out the scanners to the other companies, and I asked. 'Art, what about us?'"

"I didn't think you would be here, Jim, so I didn't bring enough for you and your crew," Hidalgo told him. "That led me to believe there was something desperately wrong with Interlog," said Robinson. He had pressed Hidalgo for an explanation of why he hadn't brought him the equipment and why he hadn't thought the 1-A Rob drivers would be there. "I asked him," Robinson said. "And he said, 'I just didn't think you would be here, Jim.' And he turned and walked away. And that was the extent of our conversation at that point with Art Hidalgo about Interlog."

A few years later, in 1996, after Robinson, Wagoner, George McKay, and Tom Turner had filed their racial discrimination lawsuit against US West, the telephone company awarded a Minneapolis transportation firm a contract to cover the same delivery routes that Robinson had developed in Des Moines. The owner of that firm called up Robinson shortly after he had returned from the Denver press conference and told him he had better not be contracting with US West in Des Moines anymore, because he, the man from Minnesota, now had an exclusive three-million-dollar contract with US West to do their hauling in five states: Iowa, Minnesota, South Dakota, North Dakota, and Nebraska. He was in the process of subcontracting the Iowa work to several Des Moines companies, and he was told specifically to exclude 1-A Rob because Robinson had filed the lawsuit against US West. "I think it was racially motivated to tell another contractor, 'Don't use that black contractor,'" Robinson told US West attorneys in deposition. "And I think if I was not black, they would not have said that."

Yet Robinson kept trying to put his company back on track with US West, even after the telephone company's managers seemed bent against him. He received a letter in August 1995, about a year before the lawsuit was filed, that told him US West would no longer need his services.

The telephone company, following its Interlog strategy, had contracted with FMC Steelcase to manage its furniture assets in Iowa. If Robinson and 1-A Rob wanted to continue to do US West work, Robinson was told, it would have to work through FMC as a subcontractor. But FMC told Robinson he had to boost his insurance and get a surety bond. Robinson said he did it, but it hurt financially, and it hurt at a time when 1-A Rob was already hurting badly from the drop-off of US West work. "That's when we really hit rock bottom," he said. By September 1995 1-A Rob had run out of gas.

But how, Theis kept asking, was all of that racial discrimination? "You were asked to get worker's comp insurance. You were asked to get a surety bond. Proper licenses," Theis said in deposition. "US West changed its vendor strategy and consolidated to save money. US West hired a black contractor from Minnesota—does that mean it was discriminating against a black contractor in Des Moines? You filed a $150 million lawsuit against US West," Theis said. "And you still expected to work for them? Forever?"

"I'm saying that US West…added an undue debt load to 1-A Rob to financially bankrupt and put me out of business when the other carriers were not asked to carry the same burden, sir," Robinson told the attorney. "I'm saying that Art Hidalgo sent 1-A Rob a letter addressed to James Wagoner, a letter that should have been addressed to me, James Robinson, not James Wagoner. I am 1-A Rob. He is OJC. We are in different areas, different markets. How can you get us confused? Unless you are thinking about us in one lump sum. Unless you put all black carriers in the same bag and you don't care who you're writing the letter to. The gentleman absolutely did not care what name he put on here. And I think this was a blatant way of showing me that this was a racially-motivated incident.

"That tells me that, evidently, from the top down, I was discriminated against....I had proved to be a very good contractor during those years up to 1991. It didn't make any difference whether I was a good contractor or not; I was going to be removed from the system....I was a black contractor, and I wasn't going to be used no matter how good I was....This is why I say this is racial."

$$* \; * \; *$$

George McKay was almost a million-dollar man. In 1993 his janitorial company, Reliable Maintenance Co., in Des Moines, Iowa, posted $997,000 in revenue, including about $400,000 worth of work for US West. That year, though, wasn't even his best with the giant phone company. In 1994 he posted gross receipts of $460,000 in work with US West—at least until the work was taken away from him early in the year. He was told the company was aggregating its housecleaning contracts across its entire fourteen-state region between just two companies, yet he was also told that the new firms would be required to hire minority-owned businesses as subcontractors. So Reliable wouldn't lose work, US West managers told McKay. Trouble is, Reliable did lose the work. All of it.

McKay was one of the quieter, less forceful of the four plaintiffs who pressed the original lawsuit against US West. "A go-along-to-get-along type," said Malone. "He would sit in a meeting, and you never knew where he was coming from." That's because he rarely expressed any disagreement with what was being discussed. He'd listen and watch, and when his time came, he would express himself, but he never tried to influence the discussion and never tried to drag or push anyone participating in it one way or the other. That may have played a part in why he never really got any work as a subcontractor from the companies that took over the janitorial contracts for US West. He has said since that he felt betrayed when he lost his cleanup contracts with US West. He really didn't want to mix with the people who denied him the business after he had performed well for them and had never received any complaints from the giant company. So George McKay never thought that the reason he never got any new business from US West was that he wouldn't network with the managers who had fired him in the first place. He thought he never got new business for another reason. Put simply, because he was black.

"The mistake that they made in the aggregation," McKay told US West lawyers, "was that they did not spell out…how blacks would be included." And by not spelling it out, McKay said, the huge telephone company allowed its prime contractors simply to refuse to hire black subs. "George, we never intended to use your company," one of the prime contractors told McKay. Instead, the primes used women-owned firms, white-women-owned firms, and Hispanic-owned firms, and McKay was left begging for work. When he complained to US West officials about it, the same prime contractor told McKay in a meeting, "We'll do business some way down the road, George." But McKay told him up front, during a meeting in front of the US West managers, "No you won't. You're going to do business in the future? You just took my future."

So McKay let it go. Reliable Maintenance made $800,000 in 1996. McKay, bitter but resigned, replaced the US West portion of his revenues with other customers and turned the business over to his son, Keith, who continued to make it grow to more than one million dollars in revenue by the end of the decade. After US West merged with Qwest Communications International Inc., Keith McKay revived Reliable's effort to win some business from the new company, but his father told him his efforts would prove futile. Again George was proven correct. Reliable has never worked for US West again.

* * *

Tom Turner's PAS Communications in Olathe, Kansas, had never held a contract with US West. Turner had never worked for the telephone giant, so it was hard for him to claim he had lost business with the company, despite his joining the discrimination lawsuit in 1996. Because of that, too, the other plaintiffs in the suit against US West viewed him suspiciously, as an interloper or merely an opportunist who was willing to jump on their bandwagon in order to share in a payoff, if ever US West offered one. But to Turner, that was the whole point. "We are claiming that US West has…prevented us from performing on federal contracts that they have obtained," Turner said in his deposition with US West lawyers. "They have misled us with contracting opportunities. They have had opportunities to let us perform…[but] they have never given us the opportunity to perform. They have pretty much led us down the street and painted a pretty picture, but their intent was not to actually engage in profitable business with us."

Turner argued that he had pursued a relationship with US West for six years, flying back and forth from Kansas City to Denver, attending minority- and small-business forums in Washington, D.C., meeting and talking with US West managers, purchasing agents, and department heads innumerable times—even going so far as to set up a three-person office in Denver to court US West. All of that travel, all of that setup, and all of those talks and meetings had cost him money, Turner said. So even though he had never held a contract with US West, his long and fruitless pursuit of their business entitled PAS to a payoff, he argued. He was candid about it. He wanted to get some of his money back.

Turner was not poor. His business was consistently making more than one million dollars in revenue without US West being part of it. In 1996, according to his tax returns, Turner paid himself $162,500 on revenues of $1.175 million at PAS. His 1995 tax return shows a little over a million in sales, too, but he also paid himself a little less salary. When he was being deposed in June 1997, he told the US West lawyers that the year so far had not been as strong as 1996, but that he still expected to post revenues of at least one million dollars. In the past PAS had worked as a prime contractor for Southwestern Bell, installing equipment and providing more than one million dollars in services over a three-year period, and for AT&T for about the same money over about three to five years. He helped fund the lawsuit, picking up expenses for the plaintiff's lawyer's trips to Denver.

During a deposition, when Theis asked Turner whether he was seeking an altruistic outcome by joining the litigation, he responded, "Absolutely not." His concern, Turner testified, "was to seek some damages for the lack of sincerity, the amount of money that I had spent trying to obtain contracts, interference with me in trying to obtain contracts. For example, when I would go out competing with US West for federal business or private-sector business, there were always disparaging comments left with the purchasing agents about minority contractors or PAS."

That kind of comment nearly railroaded one job PAS undertook for the federal government. It was an installation of a PBX system at Offutt Air Force Base south of Omaha, Nebraska. Turner's marketing manager, Steve Vaupell, heard about the contract at a business meeting in Omaha and suggested that PAS work with US West to get the job. But US West was already doing most of the telephone work at the base, and when Turner told Vaupell that PAS should pursue the job as a prime contractor rather than as a sub for US West, PAS suddenly became a competitor of US West, not a partner.

"So we made an offer, and US West made an offer," Turner told the attorneys. "Our offer was more appealing to them. And then things started happening. The [government] purchasing agent started getting calls from US West saying that we were not capable. Col. [Joseph] Laposa was getting calls saying that we could not do the job, and he went to the purchasing agent and asked her why she 'would pick an inferior company to do work on his base.' But the purchasing agent told the colonel she had already worked with PAS on a contract in New York, during the Gulf War, and the company had performed very well. That was a million-dollar project, and we did an excellent job, and she was our contracting officer on that job, so she knew we were capable," Turner said. But then the base got a letter from Nortel Networks claiming that

PAS was not a qualified distributor of its products. Turner was incredulous. He called Vaupell. "Steve," he said, "Can't we purchase the switch?" Sure, Vaupell said, so Turner told him to get a letter from Nortel confirming PAS's competency. In doing so, the company learned that the first letter sent to the base by Nortel had been sent at the instigation of a US West employee. Then George McKay told Turner that the man who sent the letter routinely disparaged black contractors. "This is business as usual for him when a minority contractor is involved," Turner told the lawyers during his deposition. "But you did get the Offutt job," the attorneys countered. "Well, we didn't get the job because we didn't fight," said Turner. "We had a lot of support from the federal government to get that job....It wasn't a situation where they didn't have to go to the mat for us."

But Turner had long been familiar with the way US West and its predecessors treated blacks. "Is there anything that you have ever heard or been told or seen," Larry Theis asked, "that would suggest to you that someone at US West does not want to work with you because you are an African American?"

"I would say I have known that since I was eight years old," said Turner.

"With regard to US West?" the lawyer asked.

"Mm-hmm."

"Why is that, sir?" demanded Theis, offended. How on earth could someone feel discriminated against by US West since childhood? The Baby Bell didn't even exist when Turner was a child, although Mountain Bell, one of the units of telephone giant AT&T, served the region.

"Because my father was an employee of US West, and so was I," said Turner, who had been a computer programmer and a manager in the telephone company's information services unit for ten years in the seventies and early eighties. His dad had worked for US West's predecessor companies for thirty years as a janitor, auto mechanic, and telephone technician. "When I was eight years old," he said, "my dad took me to the garage to ask for a fair opportunity to participate in the overtime that was being presented to the white employees....And he was told that if there were going to be any overtime opportunities, it would be for the white employees, and that if he needed money to raise his family, they understood he had some rental property [and] that he should sell it."

As for himself, Turner said, "Generally, I was told that black contractors like myself who seek opportunities so that we can stay viable, so we can have a profitable bottom line, were not getting opportunities. In other words, companies that need to generate at least a million in revenue to stay in business, we don't tend to be able to get large contracts. And when I say, 'large contracts,' I mean anything over $50,000....It was implied to me that if I were looking for a $2,500 contract or a $1,000 contract, that was a possibility. But if I was looking at putting in a PBX or doing a large cabling project, that was not a possibility."

CHAPTER THREE

Feeding the Lions

R uss McGregor really wasn't a very likeable guy, but he could talk a good game. "We were fed to the lions, sir," he told US West lawyers when he was deposed. "If you have a policy that you claim is to include minority contractors, and you recruit minority contractors, African-American contractors, into that plan and then, after they're in that plan, you feed them to the lions, that's race based," McGregor said. "We were fed to the lions." McGregor was black, a former employee of US West who struck out on his own, turning an office-products company he owned into a technology company, selling computers, parts, and maintenance services to big companies like Xerox, US West, and Lucent Technologies.

By the time McGregor made his little speech to the US West lawyers, however, he felt like he had been chewed up and spit out by the lions of the telephone company—particularly one lion, US West Chairman Dick McCormick. McGregor knew McCormick from the time they had both worked in Omaha, where McCormick was an executive of Northwestern Bell and McGregor was an up-and-coming technician. McGregor's talent with computers and the high-end digital technology that the telecommunications industry was slowly adopting attracted the attention of his bosses. He won an award for innovation and met Northwestern Bell's senior executives—including McCormick—at the Broadmoor, a swank hotel in Colorado Springs, where he received the award at a company meeting. It was the eighties, and after McGregor got back to Omaha, when he saw Dick McCormick in the halls at their office, the senior official would wave and smile and

sometimes stop to ask how McGregor's work was going. That was before Northwestern Bell became part of US West in 1984, when the
Baby Bells were broken off from monopoly giant AT&T. When that
happened, McCormick moved with Jack McAllister, the first chairman
of US West, to Denver, the telco's new headquarters.

Jack McAllister was an advocate for minorities at US West, both for
the company's minority employees and for minority-owned companies
that did business with US West. In Denver, McAllister had created a
task force of local minority business owners to suggest to US West officials how to increase the number of women-owned and minority-owned
businesses doing business with the company, vendors who could join
US West's supplier corps, which did four billion dollars worth of work
for US West across its fourteen-state service area. Herman Malone, already active in the Colorado Black Chamber and interested in doing
business with US West, chose not to join the task force, but Ron
Montoya, a Denver businessman who later became chairman of the US
Hispanic Chamber of Commerce, signed on. The task force made a
series of recommendations to US West. With those recommendations
in hand, the telephone company wrote a minority-and-women-busi-
ness-enterprise policy, an MWBE program, a policy that stated US West's
goal to hire more women- and minority-owned businesses as suppliers.
US West also hired staff to recruit those small businesses, and in its
MWBE policy statement it said that US West would act as a mentor to
those vendors, not only awarding them contracts and work, but also
providing business expertise and advice on how to operate and grow
their businesses into viable concerns, companies that could withstand
an economic downturn or even the loss of US West's business with
them. The US West MWBE program wasn't designed to build up companies so they could fail. McAllister wanted MWBE companies to
succeed and spread their wealth in the communities where US West
operated, from Omaha to Seattle, Phoenix through Denver to Minneapolis. Plenty of black and Hispanic telephone customers bought their
telephone service from US West in that broad territory. Hiring black-,
Hispanic-, and Asian-owned firms, as well as women-owned firms,
showed that US West was committed to bettering those communities

across the West—payback, as it were, for their being loyal telephone customers.

Dick McCormick was Jack McAllister's junior, but he was definitely pegged as a potential McAllister successor. That's why McGregor valued his relationship with McCormick and considered McCormick an advocate for him inside the giant company. "He knew that I had done good work," McGregor told US West's lawyers. "That was a good thing."

"And did he continue that advocacy after you left and formed your own company?" Larry Theis asked McGregor. "Yes, I thought he did," McGregor said. "He was willing to write letters on my behalf to his president of purchasing and also to other businesses in town, introducing me to the business community and encouraging them to do business with me."

But while McCormick was willing to get behind McGregor in 1993, other blacks both in and outside the company were seeing something quite different in the leadership McCormick offered US West. Most black business owners who had worked for US West or its predecessors for many years date losing their business with the company from the year that McCormick stepped up to chairman, succeeding McAllister in May of 1992. Herman Malone, who was the largest black contractor in US West's vendor corps, selling as much as ten million dollars a year in product to US West, began to experience the same things that other black contractors across the West and the Midwest later reported. His contract to supply plastic conduit to US West construction sites was in trouble, or seemed to be. He was getting all kinds of flak from US West. The company's managers wanted to audit his performance, and they were thinking about changing the way they were doing business with all their suppliers. In September 1992, Malone got a letter from US West that warned him it might even terminate the contract it had with RMES earlier than June 1993, its original expiration date. But by then, Malone had already poured thousands of dollars into setting up materials-distribution centers in Denver, Phoenix, and Minnesota to service his contract with US West. "We were shocked," he said of the letter. "I mean it was devastating news—not only to myself but to the staff. It was very deflating from a morale standpoint. It was not a good time."

Yet Malone, like McGregor who thought he had a friend in McCormick, was convinced US West was his mentor and partner. In 1988, he stood with the governor of Colorado, Roy Romer, and US West officials to announce his first contract with US West, an outcome of his knowledge of the advisory committee that US West had formed to do business with some minority business owners as part of its newly developed diversity policy. McAllister wanted proven minority business owners to be a part of the initial implementation. Malone's company, with a preexisting reputation for excellent service, fit the bill perfectly.

While Malone's company delivered conduit that first year, he studied US West's operations, its procurement of conduit and innerduct, the plastic pipe that encased the fiber-optic cable that was laid in the ground to connect one new telephone customer to another. Carlon, US West's primary conduit manufacturer, was causing a multitude of problems for the telephone company. It delivered product straight to a job site, but US West's construction people sometimes failed to order enough product to complete the work at the site, or Carlon missed a delivery, or it delivered the plastic pipe to a construction site where it sat out in the open, exposed to rain and snow, which made it brittle and eventually unusable. If Carlon made an emergency shipment, it charged more for the product, and it raised its prices almost at will, causing consternation among US West's construction project managers.

Malone thought he could provide a better service and help save US West a lot of money. He proposed expanding his contract to include innerduct, the inside-the-pipe compartments for the cable, and he suggested that US West agree to let him serve as a distributor of both innerduct and conduit across the huge US West service region. That would require warehousing facilities in Phoenix, Portland/Seattle, Minnesota, and, of course, Denver, where he could aggregate the materials—conduit, innerduct, and the glue that held the pipes together, as well as specialty products like connectors and elbows, short and long lengths of the pipe, often needed on a "right-now" basis at the job sites where US West was putting in new services in the fast-growing states of the West. Malone's own employees and US West's contract officers went back and forth on the idea. MWBE people loved it, but corporate network managers, supervisors, and construction-crew bosses, who were responsible for installing the new pipes and wires for the expanding company, were not as enthusiastic. In fact, at one meeting of US West managers, one manager asked the US West contract officer who was handling Malone's proposal why a black contractor was even being considered as a supplier of innerduct. Mark Reitz, Malone's contract officer at US West, testified about that manager at Malone's trial of his discrimination lawsuit: "He said, 'Gee Mark, I don't understand why you're pushing these opportunities for black contractors like this. You can let the blacks have janitorial contracts, let them have office supplies, but this is important,'" Reitz said. "He was smiling at the time and just shaking his head....I walked out of the room."

* * *

Cal Erwin was an Omaha trucker who also knew McCormick when the Northwestern Bell and then US West executive was rising through the ranks of the telephone company. Erwin Trucking Inc., Cal Erwin's first company, held over-the-road hauling authority from the Interstate Commerce Commission, and the company had become fairly well known among Omaha business people as a reliable shipping outfit. Erwin told US West attorneys that Northwestern Bell's shipping managers in Omaha came to him during the early 1980s and told him that one of their regular carriers was stealing from the company. They asked if Erwin would be interested in doing some work for them. Soon, about 50 percent of Erwin Trucking's work was US West business, Erwin said in depositions. Then, in 1984, he created Erwin Transfer Inc. in order to obtain proper insurance to continue doing the US West work. Shortly afterward, Erwin Transfer, a short-haul carrier, was doing as much as $175,000 worth of shipping for the telephone company. By 1988, after US West started using Erwin Transfer to help move whole offices— furniture and equipment—from place to place in Omaha, Cal Erwin's company was doing $500,000 a year worth of business with US West. A half million dollars!

It was about then, though, that it all began to fall apart. Erwin's work came through the dispatcher at US West's Shasta terminal in Omaha. The Shasta terminal's former regular shipper, the one managers accused of falsely billing US West for hauling freight it never shipped, still had close ties to the people at the Shasta docks. In fact, the terminal manager at Shasta was said to play golf "almost every other day" with the owner of that company, Erwin told US West's lawyers. That twenty-year relationship with US West and Northwestern Bell was hard to break up. Supervisors at Shasta would still call the company at the drop of a hat. During depositions, Erwin told the lawyers from US West that he complained about that once to McCormick, who was then a vice president and active with the Omaha Chamber of Commerce at the time. McCormick was discussing with Erwin and a small group of other members of the chamber how to increase work done by minority-owned companies in Omaha, but the group was even having trouble convincing the chamber's staff that the issue was important enough to make a chamber priority. Erwin, visiting with McCormick in his office one day, told the US West exec to pick up the phone and ask his terminal dispatchers whom they would call to move the desk McCormick was sitting at from his office. McCormick placed the call and was told straight away that the dispatchers would call Erwin's rival and that the desk would be moved directly. Erwin told US West lawyers: "I'm the first black in Nebraska that ever met with Dick McCormick. Dick McCormick always basically called me, especially when he had functions he needed to go to. When he needed to go to the country club with a black face, Dick McCormick always called me."

✳ ✳ ✳

McGregor never wanted to work for US West. He told the company's lawyers that he turned down the first overture US West's managers made to him. It was shortly after he left the company in 1992 to run American Office. The managers wanted American Office to work in Omaha as a subcontractor to a Denver office supplies company that held a primary contract with US West. But McGregor didn't like the idea of working as a subcontractor. The supplier that held the contract was said to be owned by a white woman, but many people in Denver suspected its status as a woman-owned business. Many thought the nominal owner, the wife of the white male entrepreneur who actually founded and operated the company, was put up as a front in order to qualify the company for MWBE contracts. Besides, when McGregor looked at the deal, he decided it couldn't really help him expand American Office further into the telecommunications technology sector. That's where he wanted to go, not office supplies. The office supplies business that McGregor and his sister did in Omaha wasn't much more than a stationery shop, he told US West lawyers. When he quit US West to develop that business, he intended for American Office to become a high-tech company, a computer services company. That's why, when US West made a second run at American Office, when the work proposed was work on US West's computers, he took the offer—that and because the offer came through his friend Dick McCormick, who was by then chairman of US West, McGregor's advocate.

With an advocate who ran the company, McGregor thought, how could you go wrong?

CHAPTER FOUR

The Frying Pan

The conference rooms and spacious hallways of the Adams Mark Hotel were brightly lit, streaming with black business owners and their wives, reporters, organizers, and speakers, who were all part of the fifth annual meeting of the National Black Chamber of Commerce. The conference was being held in Denver, home of Herman Malone, a former chairman and founding member of the Colorado Black Chamber of Commerce and the current chair of the National Black Chamber. Oddly, his local chamber was not officially hosting the national meeting, although many of the Colorado chamber's volunteers were helping usher people about and swelling the ranks of the conventioneers.

The initial sessions of the conference were running late. Malone, chuckling, told a reporter, "We're operating on CP time." Colored-people time always runs late, he said. When the conference began, author and publisher Jawanza Kunjufu told two hundred delegates that it was time for an economic revolution among African Americans. Shaquille O'Neal, Michael Jordan, and Patrick Ewing needed to start demanding to be made part of the deals that were spawned from their stardom in the National Basketball Association, Kunjufu said. The players were millionaires many times over, and they, like all of the rest of black America, needed to start spending money with their own people. "We're the only consumers of black hair-care products," Kunjufu told the delegates. "And we don't control the industry. We talk black, but we don't spend black." That was August of 1997.

In June, one year after Malone's National Black Chamber filed a discrimination lawsuit against regional telephone company US West, lawyers for the black plaintiffs had begun taking depositions from the parties involved in the case. That deposition process, too, was behind schedule, but the chamber and its plaintiffs had been forced to fire their first attorney, Eric Vickers, ten months after the suit was filed because personal and professional problems, complaints about his performance, and a spiral of personal chaos in his life had begun to overwhelm him, causing him to lose track of the National Black Chamber lawsuit. No one could reach Vickers. He had failed to notify the plaintiffs of the first round of depositions in the suit, allowing US West lawyers to prepare for the sessions only to arrive at a designated deposition site to find no one from the other side. Judges don't look kindly on such misbehavior, and Malone and Alford knew, when they found out what had happened, that they were not making a good impression on the federal court. Still, both of them figured US West would want to settle with the blacks in any case, to avoid the bad publicity of another Texaco-style racial discrimination case, which made headlines in 1996 shortly after the black contractors filed their own lawsuit, and which gave Jesse Jackson a six-month platform to criticize corporate mistreatment of black employees.

So they hired a new lawyer, a white Harvard law school graduate whom Alford knew from Indiana, his home state. Daniel Robert Webster went by Bob in order to avoid playing the Daniel Webster card too strongly, but he was a man who knew the advantage of holding the card and hoped his own eloquence would count for something in the world of the federal courthouse, where he did much of his work. He had also done some civil rights work, and when he did a little research on the National Black Chamber's lawsuit, he couldn't find anyone who had ever pressed such a suit. The claim of business vendors that a large, rich company—which as a corporation stood in the eyes of the law as if it were an individual citizen of the United States, with all of a citizen's individual private rights and responsibilities—had discriminated against a class of people, black contractors on a large scale, was unique. Like at Texaco, many groups of black employees had pressed claims that the companies where they worked had discriminated against them by treating them differently from other employees. But no one, as far as Webster

could find, had ever accused a company with national scope of eliminating a class of people from the ranks of its subcontractors for racial
reasons. That's what the black business owners' lawsuit claimed. With
Texaco going down for $176 million, Webster saw US West, a regional
Baby Bell capitalized at about $40 billion, settling for big bucks rather
than facing the explosive discrimination charges of a few black janitors,
truck drivers, and high-tech wannabes.

"We'd like to work something out so that we can resolve this matter
without litigation," a spokesman for US West, David Biegie, told the
press when the depositions began. But even by the time of the National
Black Chamber convention, just two months after those depositions
had started, it was clear the company was playing hardball in federal
court. It didn't want its chairman, Dick McCormick, or Sol Trujillo, its
president and chief executive officer, to testify in the National Black
Chamber case, not only because the executives were busy men who had
enough to do to keep US West making as much money as it did—$1.2
billion in '94, $1.1 billion in '95, and $1.3 billion in '96—but also
because McCormick and Trujillo, the company's lawyers said, were too
high up the executive ladder to have had any direct impact on the MWBE
program. They read reports of its results, but that was all. Other people
were responsible for how the policy was enforced. Besides that, the company was engaged by then in a campaign to improve its image among
minority consumers, an effort that followed the filing of the blacks'
lawsuit and a campaign that seemed aimed directly at refuting his claims.

The Black Chamber's suit, even if it hadn't gone anywhere yet, was
a burr under the saddle of McCormick's and Trujillo's leadership of the
company. Jesse Jackson had already caused Texaco a great deal of pain
and cost it a great deal of money. US West, which also was being bat-
tered by the press at the time for poor service, could ill afford a
Texaco-type case exploding into national headlines. Besides all that,
Trujillo was Hispanic. He had worked very hard to include Hispanics
in US West's business consideration, and he hated having another ethnic minority group accusing the company of racism. In November of
1996, shortly after the Texaco settlement broke, Trujillo had made sure
the press took note that US West had signed on a Hispanic company to

provide it with eight million dollars worth of telephone assemblies for two years and a black-owned firm to provide it with paper and office supplies for a year at $400,000. It didn't matter that the $400,000 didn't match the $8 million nor that some people in the black business community in Denver questioned the validity of the black ownership of the office supply firm. The contracts, US West said, were part of $350 million being spent with women- and minority-owned firms in 1996. What were those black businessmen talking about?

* * *

Herman struck up a conversation with Sandra Mann, the office manager for the Greater Metropolitan Denver Ministerial Alliance, at Pierre's, a restaurant and bar in Northeast Denver famous for its fried catfish that served as an after-work gathering place of the city's middle-class African-American community. It was early 1998, and Malone was griping about some of the flack he was receiving in the community for taking on US West, a company that had given many Denver and Omaha blacks good jobs over the years and regularly contributed good money to black community organizations. Malone, whose term as chairman of the National Black Chamber had expired by then, had also filed a motion to join the lawsuit, along with two other new plaintiffs, Cal Erwin and Russ McGregor. In court, US West—in the midst of its minority-targeted publicity campaign—said it would oppose those motions to allow the three new plaintiffs to join the lawsuit.

Mann told Malone at Pierre's that he must—*he simply had to*—get Denver's black ministers behind his cause. She said she could put Malone on the Ministerial Alliance's agenda for its next scheduled meeting. And she did. Afterward, the ministers voted unanimously to support the black plaintiffs. At a press conference, two of Denver's leading black ministers, the Rev. Acen Phillips and the Rev. Patrick Demmer, stood before reporters with other black ministers to give their support to Malone and the other black businessmen battling US West. "The Greater Denver Ministerial Alliance would like the company to know," Demmer said, "that we are in full support of the black members of the community who have filed a lawsuit against US West."

David Biegie, the US West spokesman, said company officials were "totally baffled" by the ministers taking a position on the lawsuit and making their views public before news cameras. Biegie said company managers had met with the ministers just the week before their press conference, and the US West people had walked away from the meeting thinking the ministers were satisfied the company was trying to reach a broad settlement of the lawsuit, one that would commit US West to providing more work for minority-owned and women-owned firms. But during the week it met with the ministers, US West had also labeled the plaintiffs as simple fortune seekers. In public statements to the press, Biegie as much as said the black business owners were trying to extort money from US West's deep pockets. But Demmer and Phillips told reporters the plaintiffs were entitled to cash settlements. Phillips said he considered the ten million dollars in damages sought "small dollars." He said he and other black leaders also were among the people who met with Trujillo before the black businessmen's lawsuit was even filed. They had walked away from that pre-lawsuit meeting, they said, fairly confident that no suit would be necessary to satisfy the black business owners' grievances with the telephone company. "I don't know how it fell apart between that time and this time," said the Rev. Phillips.

✳ ✳ ✳

Malone needed a minister by then. His life was falling apart. His business was failing. He was arguing with his wife Pauline, the love of his life. His company was under fire. Losing US West's conduit contract forced him to lay off nearly half of his employees, including Pauline, who had been working with the company ever since she and Herman had married in Washington, D.C., in 1992. The black plaintiffs in the lawsuit had won the right to depose McCormick and Trujillo, but US West's attorneys also tried to silence the black men by asking a US magistrate who was handling the preliminary legal steps in the case to issue a gag order that would have kept the press from continuing to report on it. Malone had been deposed in January during a contentious, all-day meeting with those same US West lawyers, where Malone was forced to recount the dramatic drop-off in business at RMES during the first year of his marriage. From 1993, when the company posted $11.7 million in sales—mostly its conduit work with US West—his business dropped to just $2.7 million in 1994, $1.2 million in 1995, and less than that in 1996. Serving as chairman of the National Black Chamber gave Malone national standing in the Colorado black community. The ministers did come to his aid, and other people looked up to him and admired his taking on US West. But others in the black community bitterly resented him for making trouble. The Colorado Black Chamber, led by former US West executive Bob Patton, refused to host the National Black Chamber's convention, partly because the national chamber, led by Malone, had gone ahead and filed the lawsuit despite Patton's reticence to attack a powerful source of the local chamber's funding. Many of the volunteers who helped Herman organize the National Black Chamber's convention were also loyal and active members of the local chamber, but US West—an early supporter of the National Black Chamber—was conspicuously absent from its list of sponsors for the Denver convention. The national chamber's lawsuit, the depositions, and public backbiting between the plaintiffs and US West in the press had a lot to do with US West's absence.

CHAPTER FIVE

The Fire

D Robert Webster realized quickly that federal Judge Wiley Daniel had come to the hearing prepared. Because the case had "seemed to languish for a long period of time," said the judge, "I want to review." Then he launched into a twenty-minute recap of the two years it had taken to get to that March day's court session. Daniel needed to decide whether the lawsuit truly represented a claim relevant to all black business contractors in the fourteen states served by US West's telephone system, or whether the claim was relevant to none of those contractors or relevant just to the four companies that had filed the lawsuit. Then there was a new issue of whether to allow three new plaintiffs to join the case. Some depositions had already been taken, and Daniel knew that allowing new plaintiffs to join the case would prolong it even more and that US West's lawyers would need more time to prepare a defense against the new claimants.

Daniel also personally knew one of the prospective new plaintiffs, Herman Malone. Denver's black community was not very large, and it was close-knit. Daniel had played golf with Malone and knew of his activism and reputation for leadership in the black business community. What Daniel could not understand now was how poorly the black plaintiffs' case had been put together. Webster was asking him to certify the case as a class action, yet the court papers Daniel had studied before the hearing described no size of the class, no numbers of businesses that could have been hurt by US West's alleged discrimination, and no evidence that anyone other than the plaintiffs had suffered any discrimination at the hands of US West. The evidence, in fact, was pretty sketchy, especially since one of the company plaintiffs had never done any work at all for US West. How could US West have discriminated against that plaintiff if the plaintiff's company had never even done any work for the telephone company? The case also failed to show how the National Black Chamber of Commerce, a named plaintiff, had suffered any damage at all as a result of US West's supposed discrimination. Daniel's court district, the community of federal judges who ran the court, had strict rules for allowing certification of a class, and this white lawyer before him, Daniel thought, this supposed civil-rights fighter named Daniel Webster, had filed nothing to suggest he was even aware of those rules. What was Webster thinking? That Wiley Daniel was going to roll over for him because four black business guys were claiming that big, rich US West had done them wrong? No way! Wiley Daniel was going to be as meticulous as he always had been on the bench; that's what had gotten him there. He was determined that the black businessmen were going to have to prove their case beyond a doubt, and he knew, being black himself, that it was hard to prove racial discrimination claims in courts in the West. Jurors just had a hard time going there, and lawyers could never seem to present a case that clearly, indisputably documented motive: a desire to hurt someone purely based on the victim's race.

Racism was much easier to prove in criminal court, where injury or death was undeniable. In civil court you have to prove financial harm—harm to someone's reputation or business life that had measurable financial consequences. In the minds of western jurors—minds forged by rock and river and wind—Judge Daniel knew that victims were held just as accountable for their actions as the people hauled into court for harming those victims. It was a tough environment to make a case for unspecified damages that left no visible scars. Wiley Daniel knew discrimination scarred the soul, but this D. Robert Webster, the judge thought, would have a hard time describing damages to the soul to a western jury. The lawyer's filings, in fact, had failed to demonstrate any detailed financial damage suffered specifically by each company named in the lawsuit, much less all the companies in the proposed class. An explanation of individual damages was simply left out of the case files he had before him. Daniel Webster had given him nothing much at all.

"I am confused about what the class is, who would be in it, and how large the size of the class would be," said the judge, facing the silver-haired Webster at a lectern in the well of the courtroom below him. The papers arguing for class certification, said Daniel, were rife with "obscurantism," and the NBCC, the National Black Chamber, "is not asserting that it, as an entity, has sustained any losses," said the judge. "I'd like to know if it has standing as a representative plaintiff," he barked.

Webster was flustered. Herman Malone and Russ McGregor, sitting in the dark benches fifteen feet from the lawyer, noticed that his face—normally friendly and openly composed when he spoke to his black friends and clients—was shrinking and taut, and was turning visibly redder as every moment passed. Larry Theis, US West's lawyer, seemed comfortably smug on his side of the courtroom as the judge continued.

"This affidavit," the judge said, as he waved the sworn statement of NBCC president Harry Alford in the air over the edge of his bench, shaking the pages like a wagging finger, as if he were scolding a child: "Alford doesn't supply evidence of his conclusions."

"'We feel that they were wronged,'" the judge read from the papers. "What does that mean?"

Webster tried to save himself. The plaintiffs have a witness, he told the judge. That witness was Wiley Wilson, another black businessman, who had been there from the beginnings of US West's efforts in Denver to establish a woman- and minority-business vendor program. He could testify to the class and the desires of many businesses to work with US West as contractors, and he thought that he himself had been wronged by US West because the company had failed to pay him for some consulting work.

"Well, let's hear him," said the judge.

Wilson took the stand, but he couldn't tell Daniel how many black-owned companies had suffered discrimination at the hands of US West managers. He had his own tale to tell, but the judge was looking for testimony that had evidentiary value, not more rhetoric and whining.

Theis got up and told the judge the plaintiffs had proven nothing during the hearing. They couldn't estimate the size of the class. They couldn't demonstrate that anyone who might be in the class had suffered a common measure of harm as a result of being discriminated against. "And besides, your honor," the lawyer added, "it's now 1998. The alleged discrimination against these plaintiffs, which US West denies, was supposed to have occurred in 1988 and 1990 and 1992, and the clock on such a complaint, your honor, according to the rules of this federal court, ran out on these plaintiffs long ago." US West would move, eventually, for the dismissal of the whole case, Theis said, but certainly it was arguing today that not only had the plaintiffs failed to demonstrate that a class of people who were harmed actually exists, but also that the plaintiffs had no idea how many people were supposed to be in that class. They had shown nothing to the court that suggested anyone would ever be able to count them or calculate what measure of monetary damage any of those fictional people had suffered.

Judge Daniel agreed. "I can't determine what the class would be," said the judge. Mr. Webster and the plaintiffs, he said, had failed in a half dozen other ways to prove, according to the court's rules, that a whole bunch of people like them had potentially suffered the same fate for the same reasons at the hands of US West. The plaintiffs' depositions were interesting, Daniel said. Some of the testimony in the depositions had even come from US West employees who had indicated the company was less than sincere and committed to its own women- and minority-owned business enterprise program. Certainly the plaintiffs, or at least some of them, could demonstrate a loss of business on the part of their companies when US West dropped them as vendors. Because of that, Daniel said, he was going to allow the case to go forward, but not as a class action, and he also would allow the new plaintiffs to join it. Mr. Webster, though, Judge Daniel warned, had better do a much better job preparing for trial than he had done preparing for the hearing. Civil juries, Daniel knew, could often be more demanding than even judges when it came to wanting to see demonstrable evidence of harm done to someone, especially when it was blacks saying whites had done them wrong.

＊ ＊ ＊

Herman Malone was dumbstruck. When a reporter cornered him in the hall outside the courtroom, he said he was naturally disappointed with the ruling, but that he was prepared, especially since the judge had allowed his own firm, RMES, to join the lawsuit, to proceed with it and prove that US West had done harm to other African-American-owned businesses. "We carry that burden," Malone said. But standing there, knowing just how financially damaging the case and his experience with US West had started to become for him, Malone could only hope he was putting on a good front. He hoped the reporter wouldn't be able to fathom the dark fear that clawed at the pit of his stomach just then. His business, RMES, was going under. In a month it would file for protection under the federal bankruptcy laws. He owed the IRS more than $100,000, and the state and city another $65,000. He owed $1.2 million to Vectra Bank, which had come to his aid after his longtime banker, United Bank, had called his line of credit. He owed the city of Denver $191,000 borrowed on the building he had bought to service the US West conduit contract—the million-dollar contract that his business had been built upon and that had been gone now for almost four years. Almost a year earlier, his comptroller, Steve Mitchell, was let go from the company. His son, Leon, was let go in August; his senior project manager, Sony Smith, left in October; Jesse Carter, his best friend and his project manager for outside construction, left in November; and his wife, Pauline, left the business in December. It was clear that a bankruptcy filing was in the cards for RMES. He would have to sell his building to pay his debts, and it wasn't going to cover them all.

RMES's four administrative staff (Malone; Len Murray, his vice president of operations; Chris Pate, his bookkeeper; and his niece, Paulette Malone) were managing three contracts that—along with some pay telephones RMES bought and installed at Denver International Airport in 1994 and a security monitoring contract managed by Malone—were bringing in the company's only revenue. None of those contracts made as much money for RMES as the work the company had done for US West. One contract that involved only one employee was for an upgrade of certain telephone systems at Eglin Air Force Base in Florida; the second was for telephone maintenance at the Western Area Power Administration offices in Denver—again only a single-technician contract; and the third was a subcontract with US West for maintenance of phones at DIA, where RMES had four employees. Malone was managing a security monitoring contract at the Federal Center in Denver, a huge federal office complex in Lakewood, a suburb where about fourteen workers manned the security stations and reported to RMES.

Those four contracts and ownership of the phones at DIA were bringing in almost $193,000 a month then, but it was not enough to make loan payments, make payroll for the technicians who did the work on the contracts, pay his own salary and his administrative staff, and fund the costs of moving from the old facility to smaller offices off the edge of downtown Denver. Besides all that, US West said RMES still owed it $36,000 for leases of the construction equipment the company needed to do the outside plant work that was supposed to replace his conduit-contract revenues, but never did. In fact, RMES lost so much money trying to become a construction contractor for US West—a chore that Malone told US West officials his firm could never be good at— that when that work ended and money from the pay phone ownership at DIA was interrupted because of a national legal dispute with long-distance telephone companies, Malone's company was suddenly left hung out to dry. He filed for Chapter 11 bankruptcy protection on April 14, 1998. The newspapers carried the story a week later. Herman Malone, the former chairman of the National Black Chamber of Commerce, was fighting for his financial life. And one of his creditors, one of the wolves snapping at the cabin door, was none other than the company that had put him under the spotlight to begin with: Sol Trujillo's and Dick McCormick's gargantuan and deep-pocketed US West, the minority business owners' friend. Few people gave him much of a chance to survive.

CHAPTER SIX

Standing Alone

Before Malone filed for bankruptcy protection, he and his fellow plaintiffs in the lawsuit gathered in March at Malone's plant in Denver, coming from all parts of the country—Iowa, Omaha, Phoenix, and Kansas City—to talk out a strategy for settling with US West. But Harry Alford and Bob Webster, who were supposed to be there, never showed up. The plaintiffs, all black contractors, were to meet the next day with US West's lawyers and other company officials. They had already submitted a letter outlining their demands for cash settlements, from three million dollars sought by Tom Turner from Kansas City to forty million dollars for Herman Malone, representing his lost conduit-contract revenues—revenues US West had told him he would make up with outside-plant construction work. The total was $85.4 million for all seven plaintiffs. US West responded with offers of much, much less: $352,000 for Malone, $57,750 for Jim Robinson's 1-A Rob Moving, $140,000 for Daddy Wags's OJC Transfer, and other amounts for the remaining plaintiffs. Its total offer was $1.27 million.

At the meeting the next day, the men were planning to turn down those US West offers as inadequate, and Malone wanted to tell Alford and Webster to press the discrimination case. The plaintiffs thought they had a very good case. Every one of the business contractors also knew that first offers in any negotiation were always high or low; such figures were argued up and down to a reasonable point on which both sides could agree. That's how the business world worked. They all just wondered why Alford and Webster weren't there early enough to discuss the strategy before going into the meeting. When they finally reached

Webster, their attorney, he claimed to have a family emergency that required him to reschedule a later flight. The plaintiffs never reached Harry Alford that night.

But everyone—Alford and Webster included—met the next morning at a hotel restaurant. Some of the ministers who had spoken up for Herman in February had hoped also to attend the settlement meeting at Larry Theis's office on Broadway in Denver, but when everyone got there, US West lawyers and other US West people who were there told the ministers that the meeting about to take place had to do with cash settlements for the men, not a wider, corporate response to the claims of discrimination against black vendors—so the ministers didn't need to be there. They were, in fact, turned away.

When the plaintiffs went into the meeting, however, Alford rose to speak and began to urge the plaintiffs to accept the offers US West had on the table. In a big conference room with all the US West people there, Alford began to address each of the men individually, declaring that each really couldn't afford not to accept the settlements, that they'd be doing a disservice to their families if they didn't accept the offers. He also said the National Black Chamber, no longer being a part of the suit, couldn't continue to support the legal effort financially. The plaintiffs would have to start paying Webster more money if they weren't willing to accept the offers.

Malone suddenly realized that all this was being said in front of the plaintiffs' legal opponents. And Webster, he thought, was curiously silent. He started to wonder what was going on between Webster and Alford. When Malone rose to address the group, he asked Alford why he was all of a sudden doing all the talking when the plaintiffs' lawyer was sitting there, too. Alford said he was representing the Chamber. But the Chamber, as Alford had just said, was backing out of financially supporting the plaintiffs. "How dare you!" Malone said, outraged that Alford was essentially undermining the plaintiffs' legal position. Alford was not, Malone said, turning to the whole group, by any means representing the plaintiffs. It was then that people in the room suggested a recess, time for the plaintiffs to cool off and conference together. The

US West people left the room. When they returned, everyone agreed to have a follow-up meeting in Kansas City in April.

Harry Alford, meanwhile, had just been invited to ride back to Washington, D.C., with Dick McCormick on the company's corporate jet. McCormick, naturally, was interested in the settlement meeting, and he called Larry Theis during the session to check on its progress. Theis passed the phone on to Alford, and McCormick offered to fly Alford home from Denver, an invitation Alford accepted in front of everyone in the room. McCormick was known for liking pistachio nuts. The plaintiffs, leaving the meeting, joked with each other about Harry getting treated to some of Dick McCormick's pistachio nuts on the flight to D.C. Later, the black businessmen all came to suspect Alford was treated to something more. The National Black Chamber was no longer a party to the lawsuit, but Harry Alford, they concluded, was probably cutting himself a pretty good exit package.

In Kansas City, on April 30, US West's Theis went around a conference table in an airport-hotel conference room and had each individual plaintiff once again restate why he had felt aggrieved by US West and what each man estimated he had suffered in terms of damages to his business. It took most of the morning, and after the group broke for lunch, Webster and Theis began to meet individually with business owners to negotiate a separate final settlement figure with each plaintiff and to get each man to swear to keep the figure secret, even from every other fellow plaintiff, or else risk violating their own private settlement agreement. By about three that afternoon, Webster and Theis emerged and told Herman Malone they'd have to meet with him individually some other time because they had run out of time and had to catch their flights back home. Malone felt more than a little left out, but he figured he could cut a deal from Denver as easily as from Kansas City. He didn't expect Bob Webster's call a few days later saying he could no longer represent Malone in the case. Malone was taken aback. He had just filed his bankruptcy petition in mid-April, hiring a whole new set of attorneys to represent him in that action, and pre-trial deadlines for the discrimination lawsuit were fast approaching.

Malone was determined to press his case, and he once again re-cruited the ministers to work on his behalf, meeting with them and Robert Knowling, US West executive vice president for operations, a black man himself, who had been put in charge of US West's minority-and-woman-owned businesses vendor program in October. The ministers wanted to know why Herman had been left out of the settle-ment negotiations and whether US West was going to come through with a broader settlement that would affect future black business own-ers. Knowling, who was tracking the settlement negotiations with the other six plaintiffs, seemed in agreement with the ministers. He said he was pressing US West CEO Sol Trujillo for a full settlement.

Within about a week, on the morning of July 9, 1998, both of Denver's newspapers carried big headlines in their business sections: "Phone exec quits" and "Knowling to leave US West." The ministers and Malone were stunned. Knowling was the highest ranking African American working at US West, recruited in 1996 from Ameritech, the Chicago-based Baby Bell, to turn around US West's horrible customer-service problems. The huge company was practically unable to get phones installed or answer customer complaints fast enough at a time when the telecommunications industry was booming and people by the thou-sands were seeking multiple telephone lines to run businesses from home and new, faster computers in offices that required high-speed transfer of data ranging from accounting statistics to worldwide sales. When Knowling's responsibilities were expanded to include the Minority and Women Business Enterprise program at US West, Herman and the ministers thought they would have a lock on working out the black community's problems with the company. When Knowling became involved in the negotiations over the lawsuit, everyone—the ministers, Webster, Alford, Malone, the rest of the plaintiffs—had almost physi-cally felt their prospects rising, boats on a high-tech economic flood.

But now Knowling was gone. He was moving to California and would be CEO of a high-tech company there. Herman Malone knew the other plaintiffs were still deeply involved in negotiating their settle-ments with US West. On August 8, the newspapers made it official. US West had settled with six of the black businessmen who were plaintiffs in a lawsuit that accused the company of a pattern of discrimination against black business owners—a charge the company still emphatically denied, even as it settled the six cases. David Biegie, a public relations spokesman for the company, said US West was still negotiating with Malone and would later announce a plan to address the black community's broader concerns that blacks were being left out of US West's booming prosperity. Malone himself told a reporter, "We certainly want to get this behind us." But strangely, he felt a little like he had that day in June 1996 when he stood in the sun sweating over the press conference arguments. On that day, he had stepped up, and he knew then he was putting his business with US West at risk. Two summers later, he realized, he was still standing up, facing the company, but completely alone. Still standing, yes, but without a doubt now, standing alone.

CHAPTER SEVEN

See You in Court

"Let me just tell you one thing," said federal bankruptcy Judge Donald E. Cordova, looking down at a table of lawyers from US West. "I'm not going to use this bankruptcy case to allow you to assert any leverage against this debtor....We're not going to use the bankruptcy case to put any pressure on the debtor to settle his litigation with your company." The lawyers, Paul Grant and Steven Perfrement, were shocked. Perfrement, newly hired at Larry Theis's office as Malone's business-discrimination lawsuit neared trial, had come to the bankruptcy proceeding to help press a US West request that Cordova appoint an outside examiner to take over Malone's company and settle the discrimination suit. The request had been filed the day before Cordova met the lawyers in court. At the same time, the company reduced its settlement offer with Malone, from $352,000 to $275,000. It also said it would give up its $36,000 claim as a creditor in the bankruptcy case if Malone accepted the new offer.

That day was the first time Malone had ever met Perfrement, despite Theis's long involvement in the discrimination case, and his presence in the courtroom as well as the motion to appoint an examiner confirmed suspicions of Malone's bankruptcy attorney, Lee Kutner, that US West was making a backdoor attempt to end the discrimination case by working against Malone's successful bankruptcy reorganization. "I have always assumed that US West was staying away from this bankruptcy case because they did not want to be the precipitating cause for any failure of the company," Kutner wrote Malone in early December. "Apparently, they may be trying to go indirectly through the United

States Trustee to voice their concerns so that they are not [seen as] publicly attempting to injure" RMES, Kutner wrote. Malone put it more bluntly: US West was trying to put him out of business before he could get his day in court over the discrimination claims. He didn't know then that US West was also trying to convince other creditors in the bankruptcy case to vote against his reorganization plan and that the company was secretly promoting one creditor's $1.8 million claim against him, which would surely sink RMES.

Malone had met that creditor, Andy Duke, through another black businessman about the time of the National Black Chamber convention in Denver and about the same time that the chamber's civil rights lawyer, Bob Webster, was going full steam at collecting evidence to prove US West had discriminated against and eliminated black contractors from its supplier corps. Malone was wrapping up his term as national chairman of the chamber, and US West was under fire from customers for poor performance and a huge backlog of orders for new lines and new services. Malone was considering joining the lawsuit because his business with US West, too, was in a free fall. Duke proposed forming a company with Malone to provide what most everyone in the telecommunications industry then knew—or thought they knew—was undoubtedly going to be the next new hot technology: wireless communication of high-speed data. Duke's company owned some FCC licenses and equipment, and he needed money to launch his system. Malone became convinced of the viability of the project, convinced enough to kick in fifty thousand dollars. But it wasn't until after Duke had paid off some of his back bills with the money and then failed to sign up any customers for the service that Malone realized he had a deadbeat deal on his hands and stopped putting out any more cash. US West was encouraging Duke to press the bankruptcy court to become arbiter of any claims Duke could make on Malone's business. Cordova would have none of it, even though he was bound to give Duke a fair hearing on the claims and would still be taking testimony on Duke's RMES deal even after the court approved Malone's reorganization, despite US West objections. Malone got that approval March 23, a month prior to an unusual hearing before a federal appeals court judge who would hold the fate of Malone's discrimination claim against US West in his hands for most of that year.

* * *

The hearing was unusual because Judge Carlos Lucero sat on the Tenth Circuit Court of Appeals, the Denver-based appellate court for the Rocky Mountain region. Richard Matsch, the chief judge of all the federal courts in Colorado and the judge who presided over terrorist Oklahoma City bomber Timothy McVeigh's trial, was under pressure to reduce a backlog of cases piling up in his Colorado District. Only fifteen out of ninety-four US court districts had more delayed cases. The Malone case was already nearly three years old, and nothing had happened with it since the class-action ruling in Wiley Daniel's court more than a year earlier. So Matsch asked Lucero to conduct necessary motions hearings in the RMES case. Larry Theis said he had never before, in twenty-five years of practice, witnessed an appellate-court judge conduct district-court business.

During a three-and-a-half-hour hearing, Lucero told the parties, "This is an important case." But Theis, in essence, was asking Lucero through his motions to throw the whole case out—dismiss it—on a variety of grounds. First, in two years while the case had been making its way through the courts, Theis said Malone had not actually been able to demonstrate that he had been discriminated against because he was black. Second, it was too late for Malone to be making the claim since Colorado's statute of limitations on unlawful discrimination was two years, and Malone's conduit-delivery contract with US West had ended in June 1994, two years before the National Black Chamber filed the original discrimination lawsuit and almost four years before Malone became a party to the suit. Finally, Theis said, the case should be thrown out on grounds that US West had never made promises to Malone that Malone seemed to think the company had made to him when they canceled the conduit contract in 1994—promises to make sure he got enough construction work from the telephone company to make up for the loss of the pipe-delivery contract.

Lucero had read through the preliminary findings in the case: Judge Wiley Daniel's determination that there was no basis for a class action, the existing depositions taken from the black contractors and US West personnel, and a magistrate's finding that the discovery period in the case was now closed and that Malone had no right to reopen it despite joining the case late. Over the course of two hearings, Lucero questioned attorneys on both sides closely. Malone's contract to distribute plastic pipe, Lucero noted, later went to a non-minority contractor. Early in US West's relationship with Malone, one of the company's own contract officers was labeled a "Nigger lover" in a sign that was taped over the white man's computer while he was out of the office briefly, Lucero said. "Why doesn't that support at least a prima facie case?" the judge asked. In another deposition it was clear that even before Malone got his contract, one senior manager at US West, Jim Rudy, questioned whether a black-owned firm could handle pipe deliveries, Lucero noted. "He could understand giving black firms janitorial and office supply contracts," Lucero quoted from the case documents, "but conduit and innerduct? This is important."

After the second hearing, Lucero ordered US West to produce a leather-bound document that was the result of US West's efforts in 1988 to forge a women-owned-business and minority-owned-business supplier diversity program, to promote use of those firms. Theis said the company couldn't find the document, but one of US West's own employees had testified in a deposition that her boss had had a copy of the binder and that it was used almost daily as a reference for operating the MWBE program. "I order you to produce that final report," Lucero told Theis during the second hearing. "I'm not going to let US West off the hook." By that time Lucero had already ruled against US West's attempts to keep Malone from taking more testimony about the specifics of his particular claim of discrimination.

* * *

In July 1999, when Theis deposed Malone a second time, this time in preparation for a trial, the two men knew they were in for a grueling couple of days. Theis was bent on showing that Malone hadn't lost any money to US West but instead had made millions. Over two days, the lawyer grilled Malone about whether he made a profit on the sale of the Ironton building that was once RMES's Denver headquarters; about whether he had all along, during his relationship with US West, been taking advantage of inside information he was getting from people inside the company who wanted Malone to be a success; about why he had not passed along to US West price discounts he had negotiated from manufacturers of the plastic pipe he supplied to the telephone company, but instead kept the savings for himself; and about why he kept selling at a profit the plastic pipe he had acquired for US West after the telephone company had canceled its contract with him.

Theis also asked Malone whether he realized how badly RMES was perceived in terms of its performance on the pipe-delivery contract by US West's buyers, builders, and other employees and by the pipe manufacturers who sold their product to US West through Malone's company. "Would you agree with me," Theis asked, "that in September 1992 when Mr. Hinegardner began raising the issues that he was raising about the payment issues and the service issues and so forth, that it was reasonable for US West to conclude that RMES had not been living up to the expectations that US West had when it entered into the contract?"

"Absolutely not," Malone snapped back. "Performance—it was never an issue…if you look at the thousands and thousands of invoices that were processed and delivered in all fourteen states throughout this region, constantly, seven days a week, twenty-four hours a day, three hundred sixty-five days a year, for a number of years. You have identified a half dozen or so areas in which there were problems, but 98 percent of the orders were filled on time. You know, I'm not surprised. 'It's a performance issue,' you say. 'It's a price issue. It's a process issue.' It appears as though there were always these issues regarding African-American contractors."

Later, during the second day of his deposition, after reviewing some documents provided by US West, Malone said they certainly suggested that US West was trying to come up with anything—anything at all that was a problem with RMES. "There were factions at work " at US

West, he said, "trying to set up a pattern, trying to manufacture or come up with justification, for why the contract would be terminated and taken away. And now I find out it was race based," he complained. There was "some very serious and blatant discrimination taking place," Malone said.

But Theis didn't allow Malone's statements to go unchallenged. "What documents did you see last night that indicated to you that the decision to go [back] to Carlon [the original pipe supplier] was race based?" Theis asked. "What comments were made during this time period by someone at Carlon or at US West that were racially oriented?"

The full two days of deposition went back and forth like that. Theis accused Malone of making speeches and threatened to halt the sessions and have a US magistrate monitor them in order to force Malone to answer succinctly and to the point. Malone and his own lawyer barked back that Malone's answers were based on his experience with the racists within US West who had made a target of him and that people within US West used RMES and its relationship with the telephone company to vent the anger they had with their own company for doing business with minority-owned firms. "Let the record reflect that you're raising your voice at me," Malone protested when Theis got riled, but Theis always brought the sessions back to the calm of normal legal proceedings. Malone finished the two days believing he had performed well. Judge Lucero, the appellate court justice, would review his testimony, because it would be important to the judge's ruling on whether the case would actually go to trial. Malone was both right and wrong about his performance on those two days.

* * *

Malone's testimony played only a small part in Judge Lucero's decision to let the case go to trial because the judge relied even more heavily on other testimony that suggested Malone and other black contractors faced some tough opponents in US West's camp. Peggy Milford, a US West official in charge of implementing company policy regarding use of minority-owned and women-owned businesses, didn't even know about the leather-bound 1988 MWBE policy that Lucero had insisted Theis produce. She also testified during a deposition that US West had never required minority- and women-owned firms always to work as subcontractors to another primary contractor for US West, usually a larger company that had already established a working relationship with the telephone company. And yet a contracting policy established by US West in 1994 did just that. "The court ultimately concludes," Lucero wrote, "that because the plaintiff has presented sufficient relative and probative evidence from which a jury could draw an inference of intentional racial discrimination, summary judgment is not appropriate." Malone was going to get his day in court. As it turned out, he got two days, two full trials to prove his case.

CHAPTER EIGHT

Closing the Noose

I t was late afternoon. Herman Malone had already been in the witness box for almost two hours when Larry Theis rose from his table to begin cross-examining the man at the heart of the case. It was a case that had dragged his client, US West, into court and back into the headlines, accusing it of race discrimination, a concerted elimination of all black businessmen from the company's huge supplier corps, established as standard practice in the course of doing business with US West. That was the charge this man, Herman Malone, had brought against the telephone company—race discrimination as an everyday matter, a US West way of doing business.

How preposterous!

Theis knew he had to destroy Malone—rip apart every word of his testimony for the last two hours. During those hours, Theis was only able to listen as Malone, guided by his own attorney, had told the jury his tale of woe: how US West had picked him as a poster-boy minority contractor; how US West had done as much as ten million dollars worth of business with him in a single year; how it had sought his help to win political points with the black mayor to win the telephone installation contract at Denver's new multi-billion-dollar airport; how US West then had dumped him, like a worn-out marriage partner, not because Malone was worn out, but because Malone was black. Malone said he was a victim of racists in US West's network division, the unit of the company that built US West's wired telephone network. There were people in the division who considered RMES Communications Inc., Malone's company, deserving of nothing more than janitor's work. And all of US

West's efforts to help Herman Malone were actually attempts to set him up for failure, for a humiliating bankruptcy. There was, in this witness's mind, a concerted attempt by US West to kill the company Malone had built—just as US West had killed off other black-owned suppliers, men who had come to Malone for help when Malone was the chairman of the National Black Chamber of Commerce.

Theis knew exactly where to attack that testimony. He knew how to get the jury, a good panel of mostly intelligent white people (Theis had made very sure of that during jury selection), to understand quickly that Malone had no idea at all what he was talking about. Larry Theis knew he had to convince the jury that this black contractor was really testifying to his own incompetence, not a US West conspiracy against him. The mess Malone had created for US West was a mess born of US West's sincere, even admirable, attempts to help ethnic minority and women contractors become better business owners and more wealthy people.

"Would you look at the screen, Mr. Malone," Theis asked straight off, "and tell us what Exhibit 120 is."

"It's the five-year business plan," Malone responded.

"That's the five-year business plan of RMES?"

"Yes," Malone said.

"And would you read the first line."

"RMES will leverage our minority-owned status to gain entrance into the procurement process," Malone read.

That's all the jury needed to hear, Theis thought. That was it. The lawyer knew, from Malone's very first answer, that he could use Malone's own business documents—documents Malone had signed and written himself—to show the jury this black man was no victim of racism. That would be the lawyer's strategy. He would show the jury Malone was a victim of his own money-losing business practices, not manufactured racism at US West. And Theis knew the documents he had assembled for this case would make his point to the jury, plain and simple.

As for Malone, he was prepared for this cross-examination to be the hardest part of the trial. Larry Theis was a formidable opponent. He had proven his toughness and legal deftness during depositions and the rest of the two years leading up to the trial. But Malone had been prepped for the moment. He knew he had to remain calm, not be drawn into losing his composure, into betraying emotion, despite the flood of feelings that had been running through him for a long time now, causing him to lose sleep for months—long before this key moment on the witness stand. The run-up to the trial was intense: the mock trial his lawyers held, which he won; convincing Pauline, his separated wife, whom he had thought he had lost forever, to come back from Phoenix to stand beside him and testify in his favor; the fear and doubt that passed through him when he saw the nearly all-white jury—but for one Hispanic woman—seated to hear his case.

Malone was happy to be getting his day in court. His case was the first of its kind: a fight for black business owners' rights to be free of the racism some people in Corporate America still brought to negotiating tables where small, minority-owned businesses were finally getting the chance to build viable companies—just like Irish and Italian and Jewish contractors had done before them. Hispanic and some women contractors were getting increased chances to do business with US West even as Malone's case was being heard. His performance at trial, Malone knew, would be crucial to all that.

Under his lawyer Chip Sander's lead, Malone had laid out his case. RMES was an electrical supply distributor that, when US West wanted to enlist a few minority-owned and women-owned subcontractors to its corporate supplier corps, had proposed that it could buy and warehouse conduit (plastic pipe that protected phone wires underground) for US West's construction projects around Denver. It would bid for the pipe from various manufacturers, pitting one against another in order to get the lowest price, buy the pipe, store it until US West needed it, and then make sure it was delivered on time to the places where it would be used. In 1988, the governor of Colorado showed up at a news conference where US West announced it was giving Malone the supply contract for the pipe, a product critical to US West's success in serving all of its customers.

While doing that job in Colorado for two years, Malone and his own employees realized that they could take their concept national—or at least across US West's fourteen-state telephone-service region—not only saving US West a ton of money, but making a bunch of money for themselves as well. So Malone's RMES proposed supplying two products to US West: conduit and innerduct, another manufactured plastic pipe that slipped inside the conduit to divide the pipe into channels that would segregate different cables from each other, making laying the cable that much easier.

Malone sent his own employees into the various states where US West operates to talk to construction supervisors and others to find out how to smooth out the entire process of delivering the critical products. Then, figuring that he had an inside track on negotiating an expanded contract, since he was already handling conduit for US West, Malone proposed to the telephone company's Mark Reitz—a contract officer who had helped arrange the 1988 contract—that RMES also take on supplying innerduct and create a set of materials-handling centers in strategic locations across US West's fourteen states. From these locations both conduit and innerduct could be distributed to US West's network division as needed.

Reitz had testified immediately before Malone, and he told the jury that working with RMES had proven to be his own downfall at US West. Pushing for US West to award RMES the dual-product contract put Reitz in meetings with a variety of US West supervisors, he testified, including one Jim Rudy, a top-ranked supervisor in the Network Services division. Rudy, turning to him one day after one of those meetings, said to Reitz, "Gee, Mark, I don't understand why you're pushing these opportunities for black contractors like this, because you can let blacks have janitorial contracts, let them have office supplies, but this is important."

"He was smiling at the time when he said it," Reitz said, "and just shaking his head." Reitz said he walked out of the room. Later, however, after Malone's company was awarded a three-year contract to deliver conduit—but not innerduct—to construction sites around the fourteen states, Reitz said he left his office cubicle one day at lunch and came back to find a sign stuck to his computer terminal that had obviously been printed out from one of the office's local computers.

"What did it say?" asked Sander, Malone's lawyer.

"It said, 'Nigger lover,'" Reitz told the court.

"What was your reaction?" Sander asked.

"Oh, I was…you know, you just sort of get a creepy feeling that, you know, somebody's watching you.…I can remember tearing it off in disgust and crumpling it up and just sitting there. And it was just hard to look at everybody you work with after that because, you know…somebody had obviously put it up there.…It was really pretty scary."

* * *

With the cross-examination, Theis had a fresh start. It was the third day of the trial, and he was still questioning Malone. "RMES did not have a lease on the Denver building until July 1 of 1992, did it?" he asked.

"RMES had a lease on the building…we've always had a lease on the building," Malone responded.

"Would you show Mr. Malone his deposition?" Theis asked the deputy clerk. "Mr. Malone, would you look at Volume Two of your deposition.…You were asked, 'Do you recall that RMES entered into a lease agreement with you for that property as of July 1992?'"

"And your answer?"

"'Yes, that's correct,'" Malone said, reading from the deposition.

Then Theis read from the same document: "'Was there a lease agreement that existed prior to that time?'"

"'No, there wasn't,'" Malone read to the jury.

And with that, once again, Theis was hoping to show the jury that Malone was trying to tell them one story, while the facts of the case—as Theis could outline them in his series of documents and depositions of witnesses—showed quite a different story altogether. Theis was trying to show that Malone was just as confused in his retelling to the jury about the years from 1988 to 1994, when he did millions of dollars worth of business with US West, as he was during the years he worked for US West, thinking that US West had signed him up as some sort of "protégé" company, with a special relationship that would keep him working with the billion-dollar telephone company forever.

Business was business, Theis tried to show the jury. There are no guarantees. Malone got discounted prices from conduit manufacturers but never passed those savings on to US West. Malone raised the rent RMES was paying him as owner of the RMES building and extended the lease for seven years even though he knew US West was pulling the conduit contract from him. He did that even though he knew quite clearly that without the US West contract there was absolutely no reason for RMES to be renting the space because it had not been able to forge other supply contracts with other telecommunications companies. Malone believed those other telecommunications companies were just as racist as he believed US West was racist, and yet he had not sued those other companies, or accused them of racism. Instead, Malone accused the company that had provided RMES with 60 percent of its business over the past decade. Sure, US West had not given him the innerduct contract, which would have made the five-year proposal for the materials centers profitable to RMES, but RMES had proven it couldn't pull off the five-year proposal with just conduit. All the documents were clear. Why would the telephone company expand its relationship with a contractor that had not performed up to the standards laid out in black and white in the contract RMES itself had signed? It wasn't racism that defeated RMES, Theis said. It was business. RMES couldn't do the job. The company really wasn't very good at what it said it could do for US West.

CHAPTER NINE

Not Guilty, But...

"I'm going to go ahead and read the words of the verdict form in its entirety," said Judge Wiley Daniel. Herman Malone, sitting in a dark suit, white shirt, and tie at the plaintiff's table, knew this was the moment he had waited for over the long Memorial Day weekend. The trial had actually begun a week before the holiday, and its fourth day coincided with Malone's fifty-third birthday on May 25. But he had been too nervous about the outcome to celebrate properly.

He had been waiting for this verdict a full four years, ever since that day in the sun during the press conference on the stone plaza of the US West building in 1996. He had been waiting ever since a group of the black contractors who had come to him because he was the chairman of the National Black Chamber and complained that US West had eliminated its entire corps of African-American business contractors, seemingly for no other reason than that somebody at the top of US West, probably its new chairman, didn't like blacks. He had waited four years to hear what these jurors had to say. "I thought it was going to be my birthday present," he said later. He had been that confident the jury would see the case his way.

"Section A," the judge read, "racial discrimination. Do you find...?" But then Daniel stopped. "Before I read this..." he said, looking up from the bench, out past Malone and the US West lawyers, to the audience in the benches beyond the wooden rail that separated the courtroom stage from the gallery. Those benches were modestly full on this day, with a mix of US West officials (mostly white), friends and relatives of Malone (mostly black), and a couple of scribbling reporters from the newspapers. "Let me indicate to all in the audience," said Judge Daniel, imperiously, "I don't want any emotional reaction from anybody regarding this verdict." Then he continued. "All right….Do you find by preponderance of the evidence the plaintiff proved its racial discrimination in contracting claim against the defendant?

"This is answered no."

Malone slumped a little in his chair. It was a wooden chair, polished by many, many soft-suited behinds like his, people who had a lot at stake with the reading of a verdict: companies and people facing huge civil judgments—people like Malone. It was easy to slip a little against the grain of the wood chair, slip deeper into it, like a cowboy sinks deeper into his smooth leather saddle, to better control his horse.

"Do you find by preponderance of the evidence that the plaintiff proved its negligence claim against the defendant?" the judge read again. "The answer is no." And Malone slipped a little deeper into the seat. His shoulders dropped. With each question and answer he was growing smaller, and his birthday present was turning into a big, fat zero.

"Question 7 says," the judge kept reading, "state the amount of damages, if any, which the plaintiff had which were caused by the conduct of the defendant. There's no amount entered under question No. 7." Malone was devastated.

The judge kept reading, inexorably, reading and reading, repeating and repeating, claim after claim, no, no, no, no. By the end of the judge's reading of the verdict, Malone was sitting very, very low in his chair. Chip Sander and Larry Theis were now on their feet as Daniel talked through the cleanup language of Malone's defeat. "Dated this 31st day of May, 2000," Judge Daniel said with finality. "It appears to be signed by the foreperson and the other members of the jury. Now, would either side desire to have the jury polled at this time?"

"We would, your honor," said Sander, taking advantage of a routine procedure offered any losing party in a lawsuit or criminal trial. You always poll the jury to make sure no one among the group has any doubts about the decision.

The court clerk stood and faced ten panel members. "Michelle Weaver, was this and is this your verdict?" he asked.

"This is," responded Miss Weaver.

"Seth Howard, was this and is this your verdict?"

Juror Howard replied, "It is."

"Lorretta Stockton, was this and is this your verdict?"

"It is," said Stockton, "but I did have issues. I want you to know that."

"Lori High..." the court clerk started to say.

"Wait a minute," said Judge Daniel. "Wait a minute. Stop."

This time, Daniel was stunned. So was Sander. Theis, however, seemed nonchalant. No one else in the courtroom really was very much aware that something unusual had just happened—except, perhaps, one of the newspaper reporters who suddenly was scribbling very fast.

"Is that okay to say that?" said juror Stockton.

The judge addressed her directly.

"The question is: Was this and is this your verdict?" said Daniel, knowing he was walking on delicate ground, trying to recover what only moments before had seemed a clear-cut, overwhelmingly thorough defeat of Herman Malone and RMES Communications—and a time to celebrate for US West, its bosses, and all its hired hands.

"Yes, according to the law, this was and is my verdict," said Stockton.

"All right," said the judge.

The court clerk, hesitating just long enough for Daniel to signal him to proceed, resumed the poll.

"Lori High, was this and is this your verdict?"

"According to the law, it was my verdict," said High.

Alicia Valdez?

"According to the law, that is my verdict," said Mrs. Valdez, a social worker with the city of Denver.

The clerk finished the poll, and then Daniel, matter-of-factly, trying to show no emotion although he was reeling inside, knowing he might have a jury revolt on his hands, spoke again into the microphone on his dais. "All right," he said.

"The court needs to ask some follow-up questions. Three of you—and I think it was you, Miss Stockton, is that right?"

"Yes."

"Now, when you were polled," the judge said, addressing all three jurors who had added extra comments to their responses, "instead of saying yes or no in response to: 'Was this your verdict?' you said, what, again? Let me hear what you said?"

Stockton answered, "I said, yes, but I did have some issues. I don't know if that's permissible, but I…"

Daniel cut her off. "What I need to know," the judge said, "is, after all is said and done, is this the verdict that you approved?"

"Yes," Stockton said again. "And after you…the clarification of the two issues…"

"You don't need to respond," Daniel said quickly, again cutting her off.

"I'm sorry," said Mrs. Stockton.

"Is that true for all the rest of you, 'cause some of you didn't say yes or no," Daniel said, addressing the entire jury once again. "You said, 'Yes,' and then you qualified it saying, 'According to the law.' So does everybody stand by this result?"

"Yes," most of the jury responded.

"Does anybody disagree with the result?" Daniel asked.

"Your honor," said Lori High, "one of the claims…there was not a unanimous decision by us all."

"Tell me your name, please," the judge said.

"Lori High," said the juror.

"Miss High," said Daniel, "I don't want you to reveal on the record anything about the intricacies of the jury voting. The only purpose of the polling is to establish that each of you agrees with this verdict.…So I need to ask you again, in the light of the comment you just made, is this verdict a verdict that you agree with and which represents your decision as one of the jurors on this case?"

"Perhaps I need further direction," said High. The judge was visibly exasperated, even more so than he had originally seemed with Stockton. "My choice," said Lori High, "to put the verdict on there came from the description of law that I had to follow. Because I did not totally agree."

"We're going to go off the record a second," Daniel said then, and he called the lawyers and High to his bench where they could huddle and not be heard by the audience members, who by then were sitting forward in their seats, listening intently.

"I'm confused by what you're saying," Judge Daniel whispered to Miss High. So, in your own words, tell me what you're saying."

"Okay," said Lori High. "I'm saying that I believe that there were at least discrimination charges that needed to be addressed and awarded on behalf of the plaintiff, and because I was one of the—there were a number of us jurors who had the same opinion. We were told, we were told by our foreperson, that if we were non-unanimous and could not all vote in favor of the plaintiff, that we had to award the verdict to the defendant. So that's the only reason that I...I went along with it only because of jury instruction No. 11," she said.

No. 11, she added, "states that we had to arrive at a defense award if we were not unanimous for the plaintiff."

"That's not what No. 11 said," the judge told her.

Then, again, Daniel went back to using the language he wanted her to answer with. "The only thing I'm really asking you is to tell me if this is your verdict. You can say yes; you can say no. I'm not trying to put words in your mouth. It's a question. You can answer it any way you want."

"On the discrimination charge," said Lori High, "my verdict was yes, there was discrimination."

✴ ✴ ✴

Wiley Daniel had no choice but to declare a mistrial. Lori High's testimony at the judge's bench indicated she believed that Herman Malone and RMES had been discriminated against, but that she also believed the statute of limitations had run out on his claim. But it was the small-framed Hispanic woman, Lorretta Stockton, the first juror to qualify her answer and say she had "issues" with the verdict, who believed not only that there had been discrimination against Malone, but also that he and his lawyers had proven US West had tried to cover up its illegal treatment of RMES for so long that Malone could still make a claim against the company in 2000. That left Daniel little room to dance around the lack of unanimity on the race case.

"Here's what I'm going to do," he said. "It's clear to me that we have a non-unanimous verdict as to the racial discrimination claim. So I'm going to declare a mistrial as to that claim, but I'm going to accept the jury's verdict as to all other claims because there's no suggestion from the polling that the three jurors who had questions were not supportive in a full way, in a full and complete way, with the balance of the verdict form. So it does not make any sense to the court to grant a complete mistrial," said the judge. "So what I'm going to do is grant a partial mistrial."

Outside the courtroom, Malone was approached by the newspaper reporter who had been scribbling quickly and furiously when the first juror breached the unanimity of the jury. The jurors who believed his discrimination claim, Malone said, were "very courageous," and despite the judge's instructions to seek a settlement, their belief in him suggested that he might eventually prevail. The reporter took down the quote, and it appeared in a front-page story in the next day's newspaper. Malone went home exhausted, but feeling reborn again—a lot like that black night back in Arkansas when the cops who were friends of his brother drove him by the swamp and warned him about making trouble, but then dropped him off at home and told him to pack up and get out of town. Legally, he was alive and kicking, even if he was a little bruised. Three people on this jury had recognized the discrimination he faced playing the big-money corporate game with US West. He went to sleep already wondering if he could convince a second jury of ten.

CHAPTER TEN

Rerun That Tape, Please?

Going into the second trial, everybody knew it must be more precise, more focused on the single issue at stake for RMES and US West: Did people at the phone company racially discriminate against Herman Malone and his company, RMES Communications? Chip Sander, Malone's attorney, knew, too, that his opening statement would have to be clear and comprehensive, guiding the jury from his first words through the entire trial to a clear conclusion that Herman Malone's race—the fact that he was black—raised red flags among middle management and street-level workers at US West. Red flags about the huge amount of money Malone was making through US West and about the publicity the black contractor was getting locally—even nationally— that made him out to be a hero to the black community. Red flags about the executive-level intimacy this black man had developed and enjoyed with all the upper-level bosses who ruled US West workers' lives. Red flags of jealousy. Red flags of hatred.

Chip Sander really had only one claim to prove: the claim that Herman had lived through hatred. Everyone knew, too, that this was Malone's absolute last chance to make this case, the case started by a half-dozen black contractors who all had lost business with US West at the same time in 1992. And not coincidentally, they had all thought. Not coincidentally at all.

Wiley Daniel, the black judge hearing the case, was already impatient with Malone's claims, however. Daniel had gotten in trouble with the chief judge of the Denver federal bench over the RMES case languishing on Daniel's docket for so long, adding to a backlog of the entire federal caseload in Denver. The backlog had drawn criticism from national court administrators and the national press, too. The first trial of Malone's other business claims against US West, the trial that had led to this new showdown over the racial claim, had drawn out far longer than Daniel had expected and then ended with an embarrassing revolt against the verdict by some jurors—and a mistrial on the single count of race discrimination. Daniel was not about to give the attorneys latitude to play with his—or this jury's—time again. He wanted a wham-bam, thank-you-ma'am presentation, and he wanted himself and the jury done with this case in short order.

But that was not to be. The second trial took almost as long as the first, dragging out a full seven days before going to the jury. But you could say the verdict, returned after just six hours of deliberation, was decided long before the seventh day—perhaps, in fact, as early as the second day of testimony, when Larry Theis rose to cross-examine Malone's best witness, Mark Reitz, a good-hearted man who had become a friend of Malone, but who was called a "nigger lover" and then run out of US West by middle managers in the company.

Theis, as usual, was friendly and professional as he began his cross-examination.

"I spoke recently with a Mr. Joseph E. Polechio," he told the witness. "Do you remember Joe Polechio?" Theis asked.

"Yes," Reitz answered. "He was one of my co-workers," said the witness.

"He was a contract agent here in the Denver area?" Theis asked.

"Yes, he worked a couple cubicles away from me."

"And Mr. Polechio was involved in awarding an MWBE contract to a company called Majestic Management, wasn't he?"

"I believe so, yes."

"And you questioned that MWBE contract?"

"That would be correct."

"And isn't it true, sir, that you also accused Mr. Polechio and Mr. Mike Dorton of being on the take in signing that contract?"

Reitz was taken aback. During his direct testimony, Sander had led Reitz through his own story of having been accused of being on the take by managers in Network Services, the unit of US West that had turned down Malone's bid to supply innerduct, along with conduit, to construction sites where the telephone company was installing new cable. This question from Theis, then, was certainly meant to show up Reitz as someone who couldn't take the heat that was normal in the harsh business atmosphere of intra-company negotiations.

"I don't believe I was accusing anybody of anything," Reitz answered.

But the US West lawyer pressed harder. "Sir, answer my question, please," Theis barked. "Isn't it true that you suggested to your management that Mr. Polechio and Mr. Mike Dorton might have been on the take in giving that contract?"

"He answered that question, your Honor," said Sander, Malone's attorney, jumping to his feet to object.

"Hold on," said Judge Daniel.

The judge looked a little disconcerted, as if he hadn't been listening quite closely enough. "Mr. Theis, I want you to back up a little bit from the microphone," he said.

"I'm sorry," Theis said, stepping back.

"Overruled," said Daniel. "I'll let the witness answer."

"I wasn't going to go out and call the police and have them ransack the guy's house or anything," Reitz told Theis. But with that answer, from that point onward, Reitz, Malone's best witness, sounded as if he were making excuses for himself. "We're talking about two entirely different manners of approaching an accusation like that," Reitz said. "I approached it on the up-and-up. I documented my concerns. I followed my policies and procedures."

"But you intended to imply, didn't you, sir, exactly what you're accusing the [other US West] people of doing to you?" Theis said, driving home his point.

"I didn't, you know…you know, I didn't…you know, I think the way I presented it," Reitz stammered. "I think if it had ever come down to accusing Joe Polechio of something, he would have known who his accuser was, he would have known what the facts were; it was pretty black and white," Reitz said. But he still sounded as if he were trying to justify to the jury his strained relations with his US West colleagues—the same colleagues Sander and Malone were trying to prove were racists.

Nevertheless, it was Theis who won the match point. The jury, which in this trial included a black man who had told the court he was a roofing construction supervisor, had heard the witness equivocate, hem and haw, and backtrack; and, for Theis, that's all that was needed. His case was straightforward. The judge wanted to see it that way, the jury expected it to be delivered that way, and the verdict—whatever way it came down—would be straightforward, too. Herman Malone would be found the victim of US West racial discrimination—or he would not. It was, indeed, a matter of black and white.

✳ ✳ ✳

Yet Chip Sander didn't make it black and white. Starting from his opening statement, which was supposed to be clear and crisp, Sander started telling Malone's story in terms of the business meetings that occurred while Malone worked for US West. The attorney knew Theis had beaten him in the first trial, the first time around, by using the business documents generated by Malone's own company as it conducted a variety of transactions with US West. With this new jury, Sander was determined to undermine that businesslike approach and show jurors the human suffering, the human story behind Herman's case. "This case is about discrimination," the lawyer told the jury in his opening statement. "It's about decision makers at US West who believed that a black-owned company should not be awarded strategic contracts. It's about 'the two faces of US West.'"

But in telling that two-faced story, even during his opening statement, Sander got bogged down in the facts. "What happened," he told the jury, "was the revenues dropped from just over seven million dollars when they were distributing conduit in 1993, to just over a million dollars in the next several years." Then, introducing a second contract held by Malone and US West, Sander explained: "US West approached Mr. Malone and said, 'You have a great relationship with the [black] mayor; can you schedule a meeting…and see if we can enter into a contract to do the installation of the telecommunications system out at DIA? You can have a subcontract.' Mr. Malone did that," Sander told the jury, "and the result of that was in April of 1992, after a lot of effort by Mr. Malone and US West, the contract was entered into. It was like a thirty-seven-million-dollar contract."

Malone's lawyer went on like that, telling the jury about Malone's continuing business with US West, even raising issues that Larry Theis, the US West attorney, had raised during the previous trial to the telephone company's advantage. Sander had hoped to present the jury with a sort of preemptive strike on those issues, explaining them away before Theis even had a chance to raise them—which was fine by Theis, of course. If Sander wanted to argue US West's case in Malone's own opening argument, it left Theis less ground to cover in his own opening statement. And Theis, unlike Sander, was always going to be focused and only going to be precise.

"Beginning on January 1, 1988," Theis said in his opening argument, "over a period of thirteen years, right up to today, RMES Communications has continuously had one, and usually more than one, contract with US West," he told the jury. "During the period 1988 to 1997, RMES generated from contracts with US West over forty million dollars."

The jurors, mostly retired men and women who had had careers as professionals in companies or teaching school, were all capable of discerning the significant events of a businessman's experience from the clutter of personal relationships, politics, wasted projects, and unnecessary spending that plagues much of modern American business. They could tell bullshit from reality, and they could see through the flak that lawyers liked to toss into the air between the parties of a legal dispute and the jury box, a kind of intellectual, antiaircraft litter used to distract and deflect the real missiles that the attorneys wanted to land on target in the jurors' minds.

"US West had opportunity after opportunity after opportunity to terminate this contract, but did not," Theis told the jurors. "US West could have terminated the contract, but it did not....Now, RMES comes into this courtroom and will call them racist!...As I said at the outset," Theis added, "race discrimination is a terrible, despicable thing, but this is not a case of race discrimination....I believe when you have looked at all of the documents, you have heard the testimony from the witnesses, your common sense will tell you that this is not a case of race discrimination."

When all was said and done during that second trial, the jury agreed. "Do you find by a preponderance of the evidence the plaintiff proved its racial discrimination contracting claim against the defendant?" Judge Daniel read from the verdict form. "And the answer to this question," Daniel continued, "is: 'No.'" Herman Malone's head sank to his chest. His four-and-a-half-year legal battle was over.

CHAPTER ELEVEN

Lynch Mob

Why did Herman Malone lose his discrimination-in-contracting case against US West? Lorretta Stockton, the juror who had "issues" with the original verdict in the case, said Judge Wiley Daniel failed the panel when jurors asked for his help in resolving a dispute among its members. The jury foreman, Randy Wade, a businessman himself, persuaded the group that it was required to find in favor of US West if the jurors found themselves divided over any of Malone's contracting claims. Stockton insisted at the time that the jury panel ask the judge if Wade was correct. "The judge came back with 'The law says what it says it says!'" said Stockton, still distressed over the verdict five years later. "I'm not an activist in any way," she said during an interview long after she caused the mistrial in Herman Malone's case. "But I do believe in justice. I do believe in being fair, and these people were not fair with this man."

Daniel, the black judge, told Malone and his lawyers after that first trial that, in his experience as a federal judge in Colorado, it would be very difficult for Malone to get a favorable discrimination verdict from a jury. Daniel was trying to persuade Malone and US West to settle the case before taking it to a second trial, but the judge was arguing exactly the point Malone wanted to make by insisting on "his day in court." Institutional racism has so infected the American system of jurisprudence in this country that Malone's pursuit of justice in commerce from a Fortune 500 company in the United States was stacked against him from the start. An African-American business owner making accusations against white Corporate America; a team of good-intentioned lawyers who were no match for his corporate opponent's high-dollar, first-class lawyering; and two juries that could barely recognize racism much less repudiate it; all served to put a commercial noose around Herman Malone's neck. That left only a hanging judge to pull the lever on the trapdoor, which sent Malone swinging in the wind of a harsh American business climate.

Consider the effect of this exchange, at the beginning of Malone's second trial, among a black witness, former US West executive Larry Clayton, a black US West attorney, and the black judge before a mostly white jury that had just heard Clayton testify eloquently in favor of Malone. Clayton had had responsibility for identifying black and other minority contractors who might work for US West, but he had said in direct testimony that US West's program for contracting with minority and women businesses pretty much had degenerated into a "sham" by the time he left the telephone company in disgust over it.

"Good afternoon, Mr. Clayton," said Chuck Henson, the black attorney hired by US West's legal office to sit with white attorney Larry Theis from the private, Seattle-based, international law firm Perkins Coie. Theis had successfully defended US West in the previous trial. At this moment in the second trial, Henson was assigned to cross-examine Clayton, Malone's initial witness.

"I'd like to start with your testimony on ethical practices at US West," Henson said. "Now, it was your testimony that you believed that Network [Services] was taking the [Malone] proposal and shopping [it] around after the fact?"

"I think it was," Clayton said, "to the extent the value-added features that Mark Reitz identified were then shared with others. That's the key," Clayton added.

"Let's talk about your testimony on the MWBE program," said Henson, changing tactics. "You testified that was a hoax. Right?"

"It had degenerated into a hoax there at the last, yes," Clayton said.

"The last?" Henson asked, seeking clarification. "The time that you were acting director?" Henson sounded positively incredulous that the former director of the contracting program for women and minority contractors was actually testifying that his own work amounted to a hoax.

"Well, actually during the last year there," Clayton continued. "US West came up with something called 'end-to-end' where they were going to consolidate all of the contracts....And they started canceling all of the minority contracts."

"Sir, my question was..." Henson interrupted. The young black lawyer did not want the witness going down that track.

"You asked me a question; let me answer," Clayton snapped.

"Wait," interjected Judge Wiley Daniel. "Hold on. Hold on." After the trials, one juror said it seemed like the judge often lost track of the testimony, never paying close attention until something was said that seemed to wake him up from a reverie. "Mr. Henson, I think you asked a question he [the witness] should be allowed to answer," the judge said.

But then before Clayton could answer, Judge Daniel also turned on him. "Mr. Clayton, you're responding to cross-examination questions," he said, invoking an earlier warning that Clayton should be more direct and simple in answering such questions.

"Well, the point I was making," Clayton said, "is that the...the proposal...the value-added aspects and the pricing of the RMES proposal was shared outside of the US West family," Clayton said. "That's why I felt unequivocally that that is unethical—and it is to this day," Clayton said. "And that's the facts as I recall them."

"Mr. Clayton. I need you to slow down a little bit," said the judge.

Then Henson asked: "It's in fact true that the MWBE program was a great success, wasn't it?"

"Well, that depends on how you want to look at it," said Clayton.

"Sir..." said Henson.

Clayton continued, "I think the work that Mark and I did was very successful." But overall, he added, he didn't think the entire program was very successful at all. "You've got skeletons throughout the 14-state region....You have people that will argue with you that they went out of business based on things that happened at US West," said the former executive. "So you have to be careful when you say it was a successful program."

"Can you show the witness Exhibit K, please?" Henson asked. "K7."

"You see that, Mr. Clayton?"

"Yes."

"That shows the demographics in the region. And do you see…?"

"Whose data is this?" Clayton asked.

"Sir, I'm asking the questions," Henson snapped back, just as quickly as Clayton had snapped at him earlier.

"What is the percentage showing black population out of the total population, sir?" Henson asked.

"2.5 percent," Clayton answered.

"Your honor!" Now it was Chip Sander interrupting. "I object to this exhibit. It's not been admitted into evidence," said Malone's attorney.

"What's the exhibit number?" the judge asked. "Take it from the screen. Let me see if it is or it isn't."

"It's stipulated, your honor," the court clerk said. "It's in. It's stipulated."

Sander replied, "Okay."

But Judge Daniel looked beyond exasperated.

"I don't want an objection for an exhibit that's in," he scolded Sander. "We have a number of exhibits; you need to keep track of what's in evidence. That's a warning to both sides," he said.

"Go ahead, Mr. Henson."

"Thank you, your honor," said young Henson.

✳   ✳   ✳

That scene may just as well have been subtitled, as scenes once were framed in silent films: "Institutional racism rears its ugly head."

The racial roles played by participants—acted out before a jury of eleven white and Hispanic jurors and one African-American man, himself a business contractor—must be examined and appreciated for the undercurrent they provide to both of Malone's discrimination trials, undercurrents that give substance to Judge Daniel's claim that juries in Denver find it very difficult to detect and rule favorably on claims of racism.

In this particular tableau, a black witness whose testimony initially favored a black plaintiff accusing a rich, white, majority company of racism is attacked on cross-examination by a young black attorney who is using the witness's own words to confuse the executive's recollection about what he had actually experienced more than five years earlier.

Attorney Chuck Henson uses newly collected demographics to blur the edges of Clayton's memory in a way that makes Clayton begin to doubt that what had happened before his own eyes was an overt act of racism, and that what he had experienced five years earlier, could indeed be explained away as an otherwise normal way of conducting business. And the young lawyer is able to enlist in his company's cause the very black judge hearing the case, as well as the white attorney for the black plaintiff by creating a situation that makes the white attorney, who merely senses that his witness is being undermined, jump to his feet to object to something that the judge will have to rule against, making the white attorney seem incompetent, and making the whole scene comic. Justice in blackface. Sander objects to the use of a piece of evidence he should have known was already marked and entered into the case file as an exhibit. Then he is scolded by the black judge for objecting foolishly.

What could any jury surmise? The whole scene leaves the panel to sense, rather than conclude, that even a well-intentioned, seemingly good-spirited and intelligent white attorney could get confused by the foggy relationship between the evidence and Malone's claim of being the victim of discrimination.

It leaves the sitting black judge to look down on the young people in front of him to remind them all that they had better be professional as he enforces the white man's law in his court, or he, Wiley Daniel, a black judge doing the white man's bidding, will damn well make sure they'll be professional. He wasn't going to let the reputation of a Fortune 500 company as rich and well-respected as US West be besmirched by foolish, unprofessional conduct in his court. No way.

* * *

Leonard Woodyard, the sole African American on either of the two juries that considered Herman Malone's discrimination-in-contracting claim, and who is himself now a business owner and contractor, said during an interview four years after witnessing that tableau that he believed he and his fellow jurors considered all the evidence properly and responded to it with the only conclusion it presented to them. "We couldn't find anything solid to say that there was any discrimination going on against Herman and his people," Woodyard said.

"Based on what we were told in the courtroom, we could only go by the information that related to the case. You know what I'm saying? We couldn't allow our emotions and everything to get involved in a decision....And we were told specifically by the judge himself as to how we were to handle this information and take it and make a decision on it....We felt like we made the right decision. I still feel that way today, having been the only black juror."

* * *

Yet Woodyard also complained that he and other jurors on his panel would have liked to hear testimony from some witnesses who never showed in the courtroom, even though jurors kept hearing their names come up over and over again in other testimony. Chip Sander, in his opening argument, told Woodyard and the other jurors, "This case is about discrimination. It's about decision makers at US West who believed that a black-owned company should not be awarded strategic contracts." Then Sander mentioned US West manager Jim Rudy, who had questioned whether Malone's company was capable of handling important products for US West. But Rudy never testified at either of Herman Malone's two trials.

The process of jurisprudence plays a big part in any courtroom drama. Sander knew going into the second trial that his opening argument had to be crisp and concise and that it had to undercut many of the issues US West had raised in the first trial—or his opponent, Larry Theis, would simply use them against Malone again. But Sander's opening statement left the second jury puzzled over Malone's ability to claim discrimination against a company that had helped him make forty million dollars in sales over more than five years. And Theis, using the mistrial expertly to hone his attack on Herman Malone's most eloquent witness, Mark Reitz, who had been called "nigger lover" by co-workers at US West headquarters, was able to destroy Reitz's credibility in the second trial by making him look like a whiner who was "upset" over not being promoted or rewarded for the good work he had done at the company.

Lorretta Stockton, Malone's most powerful defender among the jurors of the first trial, believed that if US West had fired Malone outright whenever its managers finally decided that his work as a distributor-supplier was less than adequate to US West's interests, the telephone company could have avoided the lawsuit and the whole public-relations controversy over discrimination that was brought to a climax during Malone's two trials. "I think that they were terrified. They were going to get rid of him, and this is what was going to happen," she said. "Which is exactly what [did] happen....Just look at how long they kept that guy going before they told him: 'We're not going to renew your contract.' That's ridiculous," Stockton said.

Randy Wade, juror Stockton's nemesis during the first trial, said five years afterward that race didn't really play a significant role in the first jury's deliberations. "I didn't ever have that tearing feeling in your gut—if you're involved in a racial issue like that," he said of the time he served as jury foreman. "I never went home at night going, 'Oh my God, this is so heavy!'"

Five years later, in fact, Wade had a hard time even remembering the most poignant evidence of racial enmity among US West employees: the "nigger lover" sign draped over Mark Reitz's computer. Wade also said he might have viewed the racial evidence with a different perspective had he known that other black contractors for US West had also been eliminated from the company's vendor corps.

"So now they have a pattern," Wade said when he learned of the earlier settlements of other contractors with US West, echoing the very words of the plaintiffs' original lawsuit, "a pattern and practice of racial discrimination." Wade also said that after Stockton announced she had "issues" with the verdict and Judge Daniel declared a mistrial, he had asked himself, "Why didn't I see this coming?"

He said he realized after the trial, too, that several jurors "had something against Corporate America."

"It was Corporate America against the small guy," Wade said, describing perspectives he believed other jurors brought to the case. "No matter what the circumstance or scenario or analogy a person might make, they always took the side of the underdog," he said. "In this particular case it was Qwest," Wade said, using the new name of US West following a merger. "And everybody on the jury had a personal story to tell about Qwest," he said. "It was like: 'Well, my sister-in-law, you know, they didn't get her phone hooked up for months!'" So some jurors took the attitude: "'Well, I can see how that would happen; I can see how that big corporation would do that to Herman,'" Wade said.

Unlike Stockton, Wade was happy with Judge Daniel's non-response to the jury's request for a clarification of his instructions. "What could he do? It would bias the trial," said the jury foreman. And Wade felt some fellow jurors, in seeking the clarification, were trying to "wiggle" out of their responsibility to consider just the facts that had been presented to them as evidence, not their own personal and emotional responses to Qwest. "Whatever spurred us to get that further instruction," he said, "it didn't change anything. It didn't allow them to bring their own personal slant to it, which is what I think they really wanted to do."

Wade said in his interview five years after his verdict, "I'm not racially motivated in any way." But the language of racism is the vernacular; it is the language people use to describe other races at the time and place they use it. And Wade, even as he spoke of his experience five years after the fact, remembered it with words that betray the silent bias that afflicts most Americans.

"It was never racially charged," the jury foreman said of the atmosphere during Herman Malone's first racial discrimination trial. "I personally felt Herman was trying to make it" racial, Wade said. "He was trying to disguise his nonperformance with the fact that this all happened because: 'I'm black!' [But] I just never let it go there," said Randy Wade. "I'm a businessman, and the evidence spoke to [how] contractually he didn't meet his obligations. It had nothing to do with the color of his skin."

The language of racism is the vernacular. It is the language people use at the time and place they use it. And five years after he handed down important verdicts in a case of racial discrimination, Randy Wade, white jury foreman in a unique discrimination-in-contracting case tried twice in Denver, Colorado, could not even see the difference between himself, a white businessman, and Herman Malone, a black businessman. In a courtroom setting, where justice is served, Wade—like many white jurors before him—placed the real blame for all he had heard about the dispute between US West and Herman Malone right where he thought it truly belonged. He found the black man guilty.

Herman Malone was right in 1996 when he stood in the front courtyard of the US West headquarters building that sunny day when three black contractors filed a federal lawsuit against the huge telephone company they once worked hard for. Nothing had changed.

And Still I Rise

Herman Malone continues to live in Denver, and he is still doing business through his company, RMES Communications Inc., which celebrated its thirtieth anniversary on February16, 2006. Even as his case was being fought out in the courts, in fact, Malone continued to work with—and eventually compete with—Qwest Communications International Inc., the successor company to US West.

The arena for that competition remains Denver International Airport, where US West had sought Malone's intervention and aid to win a telecommunications construction contract from the city of Denver, the owner and builder of the five-billion-dollar airport. Yet Qwest has continued a campaign of business antipathy toward Malone at the airport. The company's antagonism, which has served to inspire Malone rather than to defeat him, also suggests that Malone's "true story" is ongoing, rather than finished.

But the courtroom defeat of Malone's civil rights complaint against the telephone company had a devastating impact. His mental anguish, disbelief, and disgust at losing the case, the mixed reaction to his lawsuit within a tight-knit African-American community in Denver—not everyone endorsed his battle with a longtime corporate benefactor to the community—and the substantial legal expenses that Malone continues to pay off, all played a role in his decision not to appeal the two juries' decisions. Yet for weeks following the second verdict, Malone spent time soul-searching and doing some old-fashioned gut checking. He lives by the credo "Winners never quit and quitters never win," and it was that belief, as well as his deep spirituality, that drove him to write this book in hopes of serving a greater good.

It was that winning philosophy, too, that resulted in his 50/50 joint venture with Qwest for providing public pay phone systems at DIA. That contract, won in 2000, represented the first time ever that a minority-owned company served as an equal partner on a major contract that was bid within the highly competitive telecommunications industry. It was actually being negotiated just as Malone's first trial was getting underway, but Malone's insistence on equality with US West in that partnership ensured that he would never perform as a subcontractor to Qwest ever again.

Yet for the five years between 2000 and 2005, the two firms endured a strange and strained relationship, oftentimes sparring with one another privately but never allowing the tension between them to affect customer service. The two companies simply did not like or trust each other as a result of the two trials, and it became evident that they needed to separate and each go their own way. But going their own way actually pitted them against each other. After a fierce bid competition for a renewal of the same pay phone services, Malone's tiny firm, RMES, won out over both Qwest and Verizon Communications, becoming the first minority-owned prime contractor providing phone service at a major venue in the United States. Today, he is also providing Internet and calling card services at DIA, an unprecedented accomplishment for a minority firm in the telecommunications industry.

SOURCES

Rather than encumber the text of this book with footnotes, the authors decided to include a list of the primary sources of information that were used to produce it. This, then, is a list of those documents and interviews from which the narrative was drawn.

- Trial transcript, RMES Communications Inc. vs. US West Inc., in the United States District Court for the District of Colorado, before the Honorable Wiley Y. Daniel, commencing May 22, 2000. The judge declared a mistrial on the count of racial discrimination, but accepted the jury's verdicts on three other counts in favor of US West, including no award of monetary damage.

- Trial transcript, RMES Communications Inc. vs. US West Inc., in the United States District Court for the District of Colorado, before the Honorable Wiley Y. Daniel, commencing Jan. 30, 2001. The jury found in favor of the defendant, US West.

- National Black Chamber of Commerce Inc. et al. vs. US West Inc., class-action complaint, 96-D-1331, filed June 6, 1996, US District Court, District of Colorado.

- News reports from *The Denver Post*: Sept. 18, 1996; Nov. 26, 1996; May 27, 1997; Aug. 1, 1997; Nov. 4, 1997; Dec. 13, 1997; Jan. 10, 1998; Feb. 11, 1998; Feb. 12, 1998; Feb. 18, 1998; Feb. 20, 1998; March 14, 1998; March 13, 1999; March 24, 1999; April 13, 1999; April 24, 1999; May 4, 1999; Nov. 2, 1999; Feb. 12, 2000; June 11, 2000.

- Press releases and statements issued by US West: Oct. 23, 1996; Nov. 22, 1996; Aug. 21, 1997; Jan. 8, 1998; Feb. 5, 1998; March 14, 2000; May 21, 2000; May 23, 2000.

- Depositions of Herman Malone, taken Jan. 5, 1998, July 20, 1999, July 22, 1999, National Black Chamber of Commerce et al. vs. US West Inc.

- Motion for an order to appoint an examiner, United States Bankruptcy Court for the District of Colorado, filed by US West Communications Inc., Jan. 29, 1999, in re bankruptcy No. 98-14873. Third Amended disclosure statement to accompany plan of reorganization, filed by RMES Communications Inc., debtor, bankruptcy No. 98-14873, dated and signed by Herman Malone Feb. 8, 1999. Debtor's response to US West Communications Inc.'s motion to appoint examiner, filed Feb. 22, 1999.

- Memorandum opinions and orders, motions for summary judgment, RMES Communications Inc. vs. US West Inc., United States Circuit Court Judge Carlos Lucero, filed Oct. 29, 1999.

- Interviews of jurors Randy Wade, Loretta Stockton, and Leonard Woodyard, Spring 2005.

INDEX

Give the Gift of

Lynched by Corporate America
to Your Friends and Colleagues

CHECK YOUR LEADING BOOKSTORE OR ORDER HERE

YES, I want to order *Lynched by Corporate America.*

	Number of Books	Amount
❏ Hardcover: $19.95 each	_____	_____
❏ Paperback: $15.95 each	_____	_____
Add $4.95 shipping per book	_____	_____
Colorado residents—sales tax $1.46 each hardcover	_____	_____
$1.16 each paperback	_____	_____
TOTAL:		_____

Canadian orders must be accompanied by a postal money order in US funds. Allow 15 days for delivery.

My check or money order for $_____ is enclosed.

Please charge my: ❏ Visa ❏ MasterCard
❏ Discover ❏ American Express

Name_____

Organization _____

Address _____

City/State/Zip _____

Phone_____ Email _____

Card # _____

Exp. Date_____ Signature _____

Please make your check payable and return to:
HM-RS Publishing
3840 York Street, Suite 200B • Denver, CO 80205

Call your credit card order toll-free to: 1-888-838-7637
Fax: 303-839-5232

www.LynchedbyCA.com

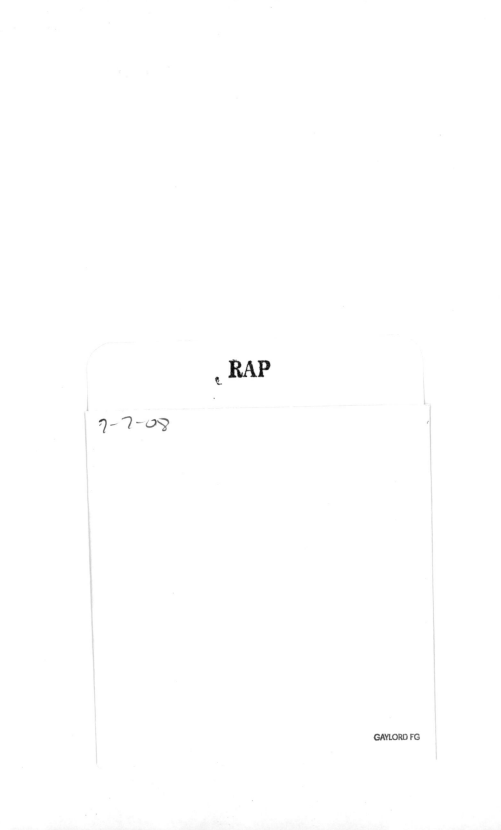

RAP

7-7-08

GAYLORD FG